Published by Little Toller Books in 2021

Text © Davina Quinlivan 2021

The right of Davina Quinlivan to be identified as the author of this work has been asserted by her in accordance with the Copyright, Design and Patents Act 1988

Jacket illustration © Holly Ovenden

Typeset in Garamond by Little Toller Books

Printed in Cornwall by TJ Books

All papers used by Little Toller Books are natural, recyclable products made from wood grown in sustainable, well-managed forests

A catalogue record for this book is available from the British Library

ISBN 978-1-908213-90-7

SHALIMAR

A story of place and migration

DAVINA QUINLIVAN

LITTLE TOLLER

Contents

When we reflect on the vast diversity of the plants and animals which have been cultivated, and which have varied during all ages under the most different climates and treatment, I think we are driven to conclude that this great variability is simply due to our domestic productions having been raised under conditions of life not so uniform as, and somewhat different from, those to which the parent-species have been exposed under nature.

Charles Darwin, *On the Origin of Species*

The Grassling bends into its end. It has listened to its fathers and mothers. It has listened to the grasses and the flowers.

Elizabeth-Jane Burnett, *The Grassling*

She was singing it as if it was something scarred, as if one couldn't ever again bring all the hope of the song together … Singing in the voice of a tired traveller, alone against everything. A new testament. There was no certainty to the song anymore, the singer could only be one voice against all the mountains of power. That was the only sureness. The one voice was the single unspoiled thing.

Michael Ondaatje, *The English Patient*

I

Passages

Invisible maps, ghosts

A monastery garden in Rangoon (Yangon), Burma 1948.

A frayed red ribbon in a pocket. Small, nimble fingers turn the ribbon over and over.

A fair-haired boy of about eleven years old is looking through a thicket of foliage and branches. His head, framed by a crown of yellowing leaves burnt by the sun, shudders a little as he bends his back and stretches his bare feet over the flaking trunk of a tree; he climbs high into its branches, light and dust particles shimmer at the periphery of his vision. He moves slowly, dodging the glare of sunlight. He slips a hand into the wiry branches of the tree, angling himself so that his entire body is taut and narrow in the canopy of foliage. He clasps his fingers around a small object at the outermost edge of the branches: a perfect mango tied with a red ribbon. He draws his hand towards himself, slowly, cupping the mango. For a moment, the boy holds the mango instinctively to his nose, its skin just touching his upper lip. He cradles the mango in his shirt pocket and then drops down, lightly, patting the parched earth with his unfurling limbs, steadying himself as if the entire weight of the fruit had tipped the scales of his body, unbalancing his being.

The boy takes out the mango from his pocket and unties the sacred gesture of the ribbon. Light settles over the thin skin of the fruit and reveals a beautiful patina of pink, yellow and amber. Somewhere higher up in the trees, bronze-winged jacana birds and bulbuls steady swaying branches. The boy presses the fingernail of his thumb down on the resistant epidermis of the fruit, dimpling the ripe fruit.

Another person might have stored up this memory of the colours, the weight of the fruit in the palm of the hand, but all this has evaded the sensibilities of the boy. Right now, the boy is thinking about hunger.

A few nights earlier the boy's uncle had stood on their veranda with a drink in his hand. He spoke softly, as if he were removing a spider from its web.

'Without a knife, it is difficult to peel the flesh of a mango. One can push into its flesh and scratch it with fingernails, but a sharp object is always required. Ripe mangoes are easier to tear; they yield, with patience, to the uneven surface of stones. Hunger invites improvisation.'

The boy works the fruit with a knife and turns its skin inside out so that it resembles a three-dimensional tortoise shell. Messily, he rips into the flesh of the fruit.

Accompanying the hunger that has brought the boy to the orchard is a small, anonymous feeling of joy. This buoyant sensation is vaguely familiar to the boy, but long since forgotten until now. The only thing the boy does know is that the fruit is a symbol; he knows this because of the red ribbon in his pocket. The boy realises, now, that he is also a kind of symbol. He knows this because he has eaten the fruit.

The monks that tended the mango orchard had not counted on this particular boy's lack of interest in authority, or ritual. The ribbons were a warning, a threat to the mortality of any human interested in eating the precious fruit that they had adorned, but the boy had felt the threat of death before, many times in fact; it held no power over him. He had grown to become familiar with his own personal set of symptoms which amounted to fear: the rumble in his chest like icy hands turning inside his ribcage, the sudden lack of saliva in his mouth, the hairs standing on end just behind the back of his (unusually) small ears.

It occurred to the boy that a strange immunity from fear now plagued him. It had first approached him gently, whispering into his ear at night, tempting him to patrol the house at midnight, hold his breath in the depths of the outdoor swimming pool, and then it led him towards more risky endeavours, lingering towards the edge of the tracks at the train station, jumping over neighbours' fences and worrying their ravenous guard dogs. Recently, he had taken to climbing trees.

Seconds, minutes pass, but there are ribbons, still, in the boy's pocket.

Sloping down the back of his throat, another piece of mango flesh sinks into the pit of the boy's stomach. Then, just as quickly as the feeling of hunger had arrived, his eyes search beyond the ruins of a wall. His gaze traces the contours of a courtyard where several other children are playing. The boy listens to these distant voices before he heads towards the shade of the stone cloisters. He runs, feet pounding against the dry earth, mud fissuring under the summer sun. The boy's thoughts turn towards afternoon tea, arrowroot biscuits and *jaggery*, the slabs of golden, raw cane sugar sold by street *wallahs* in cellophane jackets.

Just as he turns on his heels, the boy senses the mango inside his stomach and imagines it there, curdling with this morning's milky chai and porridge. A momentary stomach ache rouses his suspicions, unsettling his nervous system. Now, the red ribbons feel as if they are burning a hole in the boy's pockets. He brushes a feverish hand across his face and he hears himself make a noise similar to twigs snapping, a snatch of shallow laughter.

If what the monks say is true, the boy thinks, then I am dead now and I am a ghost running towards my friends. If what the monks say is true, then I will soon turn to stone, like the ruins of the walls of the city, like the monument to Queen Victoria in the botanical gardens. My skin will always be cool and I will be still and silent, while others breathe on my frozen face. Or, I will be a ghost, embalmed here forever.

He is suddenly aware of the fading, warm sunlight on his skin, the wind in the trees. In this short moment, the boy contemplates the sudden speed of his breathing, the feeling of air rushing through his lungs. As the boy enters the shadows of the courtyard, a question nudges him:

Do ghosts breathe?

Then, someone in the distant courtyard catches the boy's eye and smiles. Another child, smaller and with long, dark hair, tags the boy, tapping his shoulder. The boy is relieved at the evidence, the contact which must mean that he is not a ghost; even more delicious than the fruit itself, he calculates, is the thought that the threat of death has been vanquished.

He does not know why he does this, but he points to the mango trees in the garden and dares the others to eat the fruit, taunting them, grinning, bragging.

Later, piles of ribbons are scattered throughout the monastery garden. A boy's hunger has undone centuries of tradition.

Years on, the boy will think about the mangoes again when his daughter is all grown up and he is seven decades old and dying of cancer. He will know that his lungs are failing and he is unable to cease the muddling of time and space, the drifting through little corners of his unconscious. Waking moments are gauzy vignettes fuelled by morphine. Childhood memories swim up inside him like protective armour.

Armoured, he whispers: 'Do ghosts breathe?'

He enters the drift again: light breaks through branches and curling leaves. A small hand pushes back the foliage and touches the mottled, mossy bark of a tree. Somewhere else, a figure turns in a metal-framed bed, dreaming of the weight of water against his body, a dream of swimming in India.

The ghosts at the swimming pool are his audience now as he moves through time and space, out of my time and into his own; I watch his strange reflection on a glass of water.

My father fell ill while I was writing my PhD in London. My husband, Dylan, and I were living with my parents in Hayes, Hillingdon, in their modest house on a street with a chemist's and a petrol station at the end of it. It started when my father became very restless at night, waking up several times before eventually going downstairs to sit in his armchair. Then, everything just slowed down.

Dylan and I decided to move out of the house and I found myself leaving for a rural destination, packing books into supermarket boxes and rucksacks. It was a little act of self-protection, but also a form of respect: he needed quietness and stillness, two things we could not offer him while our busy lives revolved around our tiny home with two-and-a-half bedrooms and one living room. My father protested but I choose, now, not to remember the details of this conversation, or the look on his face. Those kinds of memories, they went sideways, under the carpets. As his only child, it was my *responsibility* to care for my father, but it felt more tolerable somehow to enter the orbit of his existence as a visitor from a slightly separated world. My mother would care for my father, and we would visit. I deliberately started to force a gap between life inside the house in Hillingdon and the life my husband and I were belatedly beginning together, after six years of living with my parents. Of course, I had not expected the end of that life with my parents to be so abrupt, but I should have known that it was never going to be easy.

My father had told me a story about his climbing up
into the mango trees while he was a schoolboy in Rangoon,
soon after the war had ended and the Japanese had retreated
from their occupation of Burma. He had been a prisoner
of war as a very young child and had experienced most of
those fraught years in Burma under house arrest, while my
grandfather was ordered to retain his responsibilities as the
chief of the Burmah Oil Company. My father was largely
silent on the subject of his internment during the war;
instead he talked about the latter part of his childhood, with
extra emphasis on nostalgic tales of school life – friends he
had made, cricket matches and the food he had eaten. Every
school memory was sacred. Quietly, he told me that some
boys had once drowned at school while visiting the jungle.

The trauma of his internment crept into daily life, it was
always there, like ivy twisting its way through an evergreen
hedge. Most revealing were his agoraphobic tendencies,
which he never acknowledged; he preferred to stay indoors
and he enjoyed the safety of routines. The dog knew exactly
when he was about to be taken for a walk and I always
knew when he was going to bed. He would rise early and
return to bed at 9 p.m. I knew the familiar sound of the
tobacco packet being slid open and the roll of the index
finger against the thumb, a thin paper rolled into a perfect
vessel of twine-like incense and a lick of his lower lip before
it was run along his mouth. I can still roll a cigarette, but I
will never smoke one.

For my father, smoking started at high school and
then continued into adult life where he worked shifts as
a warehouse manager, rolling tobacco while he operated
forklift trucks and watched the pallets move. After the
war, his school days had begun again, but the picking of
the sacred fruit led to my father's expulsion from the local
monastery and he was immediately sent to an American

boarding school in Darjeeling, Mount Hermon, a last resort which became his cherished paradise. A few years before he arrived, the British playwright Tom Stoppard had attended Mount Hermon, and Felicity Kendal had lived there for a while when her family's touring theatre company arrived in this region of India. Stoppard and Kendal would embark upon a relationship many decades later. It comes as no surprise to me that Stoppard wrote the screenplay for the film *Empire of the Sun*, directed by Steven Spielberg. J. G. Ballard's original story and Stoppard's experiences of war in India fused, acutely, into something which resembled the shape of some of my father's childhood.

After the trauma of war, the eating of the mangoes seemed to take on a magical significance, granting my father wishes rather than bringing about any kind of curse of death. In England, so many years later, I wished he could vanquish death again and prove that the cancerous cells dividing inside his body were simply a collective, benign threat just like those ribbons tied around the mangoes by the monks in Burma.

We decided to move nearer to where my husband worked as a professional musician and teacher in the Home Counties. I was still a student so our budget was small. I found a surprisingly cheap studio flat in a large house on an estate. The house had a stream with trout in it, a gated entrance, a marble fireplace in a communal room and a roof terrace overlooking ancient oaks and drifts of conifers bordering agricultural fields. Although our flat was up in the cramped eaves and its windows were too high to see out of, I felt I had found a good place to work and, really, its magical beauty brought some momentary happiness. I have since come to think that the experience of a place can change, unsettle the balance of emotion, thought and time, even, especially if it is encountered at the right moment. I had thought my identity was rooted in the place I grew up in, but know now how ambivalent those threads are that connect us to the exterior world.

My surname does not betray this – it belongs to my great-grandfather of Irish immigrant descent – but I am of a diverse cultural heritage, with grandmothers from ethnic-minority states in Burma and other Anglo-Asian ethnicities, including Portuguese Indian. My father was Anglo-Burmese, with a complicated ancestral heritage. While his paternal grandparents had left Coulmain, County Clare in Southern Ireland in 1885 for India via Nepal, his maternal grandparents were an unusual coupling of German and Shan lineage, an ethnic minority referring to the Hill people settled on the borders of Burma, Laos, Thailand and China. (Shan people are known for their basket-weaving skills and climbing prowess).

While my father had been born in Rangoon in the late thirties, he lived in England most of his adult life, arriving at the age of eighteen in the mid-fifties. He worked at a factory in Southend-on-Sea before settling in West London. There, he was employed as a manager at the same warehouse distribution company in Feltham for nearly thirty years where he chatted to everyone and was respected by all. I remember meeting his Indian secretary, Shushma, and a middle-aged cleaner from the East End called Trudie who was also, she professed, a psychic. He once saw a man carrying a whole carcass of frozen lamb over his shoulders, riding off on a motorbike, the dead thing and the leather-clad man making for very strange bedfellows. He spoke in Hindi to migrant workers from India and Pakistan and he spoke with a cockney lilt to men from London loading the pallets in the docking bays. He drove a forklift truck and held a licence for that which I still have in my possession today. When I was old enough, I stood on tiptoes near the photocopier machine, pressing all the buttons, and he taught me how to use an IBM computer. Feltham was where he worked, but home for him was always Darjeeling, the paradise-school. It was always in his pocket when he left for work, or turned the pages of a newspaper.

We lived in many different houses while I was growing up and I think that my father's inability to really feel at ease in England was linked directly to his desire to keep moving; it was only when I was around ten years old that we settled in Hillingdon and he began to busy himself with painting and minor renovations. I was born just a few weeks before Princess Diana walked down the aisle and married Prince Charles, a scene my mother watched while I slept and she ate snacks from the Indian stores on our high street.

A few weeks before my birth, my father took my mother for a train journey along the Central Line to Chinatown in London. They bought a whole blood-red Peking duck, spied hanging from one of the take-away windows, and ate the whole thing on the train journey home. Each time they tell this story, I imagine their fingers stained with the juices of the duck; my pregnant mother getting out her carefully folded tissues from her leather handbag and my father loosening his belt, still picking the bones. They must have looked ravenous. This was the only occasion I know of them eating bought foods from a restaurant. It was much more common for them to be given home-cooked food from my aunt in Ealing, a precious gift which was her way of keeping, in many ways, their life in India and Burma alive. They became exiles when Burma gained independence from the British Empire, despite having indigenous ancestors, so they moved to India to escape persecution: this is how Burma and India are precariously interwoven here, in my mapping of 'home'.

If there was a compass point, a destination towards

which all coordinates in my father's life were pointed, then it was his sister's simple oblong dining table in her Ealing semi, positioned just in front of the boiler in the crimson-coloured chimney breast. She also had an Indian painting of a tiger emerging from the shadows on her walls, a pastiche of Henri Rousseau's *Tiger in a tropical storm (Surprised!)*, which I spent many an afternoon gazing up at, imagining the tiger stalking across Ealing Broadway shopping centre with a loaf of bread in its mouth under the drizzly water features of the outdoor atrium on a Sunday afternoon.

We all sat around that table and watched my aunt move between the galley kitchen and the dining room, making tea and cutting sardine sandwiches into quarters. Always, at the centre of the table were several glass Pyrex dishes with a strange combination of Anglo-Indian and Burmese food that my aunt had prepared from recipes her mother had left her: *Sanwin Makin* (pronounced sinna-makin), a Burmese semolina cake made with bananas and cardamom, *Country Capon*, a chicken curry made with saffron, or mince pasties (*pustols*) and stuffed aubergines (*brinjal bake*). My favourite was the *Sanwin Makin* and its dense, rich squares of slippery, pale, banana-flavoured semolina. My aunt's apron was always stained with saffron and her hands were often scented with lemon. Sometimes, she took out a jar of *balachaung* from her larder, a spicy accompaniment to rice made of fried chillies, dried shrimps, ginger and garlic. I held my nose each time the *balachaung* came out, pungent and oily – I was too young, then, to understand this delicacy, but I always liked the illustration of a Burmese lion on the yellow label of the jar. To me, this lion was more like a Chinese dragon. The Burmese word for lion is *chinthe* and this was also the name of my aunt's favourite brand of *balachaung*.

My aunt was ten years older than my father and when she married at the age of twenty-one in Shalimar, my father went to live with her during the school holidays. My aunt and uncle became surrogate parents for my father when he became gravely ill with typhoid fever. My uncle's wages as an engineer at the Shalimar Paint Company in Howrah meant he could afford my father's medication. The arrangement of the table and the furniture in my aunt's house in Ealing must have comforted my father, recalling the configuration of homeliness in Shalimar and reminding him of the love of his sister and brother-in-law which saved his life.

It was a bizarre thing to move from London to an old house with a stream; I had never lived outside of Hillingdon, an industrial borough with arterial roads bisecting strips of factory buildings, gas towers and retail parks. Some of Hillingdon's most notable landmarks include the Western International Market, the Nestlé chocolate factory and the Old Vinyl Factory, former home to EMI Records. Suddenly I was learning about hedgerows, shooting seasons, village politics. I could walk to the village shop and not meet a single person. This rural England, the England I had read about in books like Ronald Blythe's *Akenfield*, L. P. Hartley's *The Go-Between* (via my 'A' Level in English) and Evelyn Waugh's *Brideshead Revisited*, was entering my life sideways, across the vertical constant that was my family and, back then, the writing of my PhD. I began to think about the journeys my own family had taken, and the routes they took, crossings which encompassed southern Ireland and Nepal, Calcutta to Rangoon, and the most significant one for both my parents, Rangoon to England by boat via Egypt. England was, for them, the Royal Family, Earl Grey tea, Marks and Spencer woollen blankets and Imperial Leather soap. The greenness of England and its rural palette of auburn and dirty emerald hues must have been a shock for my family as they peered through train-carriage windows on their way from Portsmouth Harbour to London. They would have seen trees continually sodden with sheets of rain, mud irritatingly clumping under polished leather shoes.

Before we left Hillingdon, my own notion of the English countryside was felt only as a residual or fleeting presence, most memorably evoked through the appearance of my husband's shabby wellington boots, incongruous in our local, carpeted pub in suburban Hayes, The George Orwell, named in honour of the author's brief employment here as a local Prep School teacher. Other than the peculiar sight of Dylan's muddy boots in the Orwell, to me, the countryside was just experienced as a flattened image behind the windscreen of our car when I accompanied him to work sometimes, sitting in a school car park reading from a pile of books. Now, the mud was on *my* boots, I was in that place he had often disappeared to and I had become a new figure in the landscape of his world, even though we had lived together for years. We had left Hayes behind, much like Orwell himself who moved on to Southwold in order to write his first novel, *Burmese Days*. As a police officer stationed in Burma, Orwell would have known the streets of Syriam as well as my father. Sometimes, the reality of everyday life is stranger than fiction.

We left behind a sense of familiarity and warmth in Hayes. There was always a kind of homeliness, in our connections with shopkeepers we had known for years, neighbours, school friends, my father's mates in the bookies', the owner of the Chinese take-away and the Tamil gentleman who always smiled, working in KFC until late every night. Everyone was 'Aunty' or 'Uncle', as is the custom for Asian elders, but even the young Somali men in smart suits who ran the local internet café greeted me as I went there every week to print off chapters of my PhD; they called me 'sister' and they even called my English, Cornish husband, 'brother'. 'As-salam alaykum', the Somali men would say to us in their crisp, ironed shirts. Yes, it was not as pretty or quiet as Surrey, and it was becoming precarious at night, but I had lived there for twenty-seven years. I blithely moved in a different direction, not like one of my dearest school friends, who left Hayes and went all the way to New Zealand to marry a Wellingtonian carpenter, but a few significant miles further West, nevertheless.

This was the start of a cadence, a measurement, by which I began to judge every other home, with my tuning fork in my fingers: *how much is it like Hayes*? The answer to this question, for the last decade has always been that each of my homes in Surrey, Berkshire, Hampshire, Devon, were vastly different to Hayes. Why is that, then? I take the tuning fork out and it sits in the air, still, its two prongs pinching the atmosphere. The answer is simple: I am not listening out for the same pitch, or cadence, I am listening out, always acutely, to the differences. These, I know, tell me exactly where home is and all the spaces in between.

After our move, an England very different to the suburban one he had experienced for the past five decades entered my father's everyday routines through our discussions. While he drank tea, played with the dog and shared the television remote control with my mother, I would tell him about trees, animals and fields, about the pheasants I had seen nearly run over, as if they were alien entities, found objects. I described the shape of the bricks in the building I lived in, the stained glass in the Saxon chapel. My father listened. Of course, he already knew about sacred ruins, and mango trees, and chickens which would be made into curries by the chefs at school, he had experienced nature and all kinds of pastoral vistas as a child, not as exotic pleasures, but as the very fabric of life in Burma and India. Now we talked about the nightjars and woodcocks which flew past the stream in Albury and the dawn chorus which greeted us from the rooftop of our building, as loud and thrilling as a rock concert.

One morning, I saw my father looking out at the garden in Hayes from his chair. He had turned his entire body so that he could see without getting up. A sparrow had circled the garden path and was resting by our plum tree.

'What are you looking at?' I asked.

'That bird over there. It looks just like a bulbul.'

'A *what?*'

'You see them in India.'

The Oxford Handbook of the Birds of India and Pakistan describes the bulbul as a small bird belonging to the Pycnonotidae family. They have long, notched tails and they can appear in colourful variations of olive-brown, yellow or brown to black. They are songbirds, keen on lively harmonies. A. L. Lintoch's entry in the 1922 edition of *The Journal of the Bombay Natural History Society* describes the discovery of bulbul bird eggs in the Nelliampathy Hills of Kerala, comparing his findings with those of the Victorian naturalist E. W. Oates. The bulbuls, or *Otocompsa emeria fuscicaudata,* had laid eggs in a coffee tree during December, a month not usually associated with the bulbul's mating season, according to Oates's *The Fauna of British India, including Ceylon and Burma.* Lintoch writes excitedly about his discovery of the bulbuls in Nelliampathy, commenting on the size of their eggs and the frequency with which they are laid. Historically, the birds always nest in the hills, returning in November; the migration habits of the bulbuls seem unpredictable, but then they are songbirds, as Oates also notes: they make musical sense out of the strangeness of the new.

Apples

A small boy, of about twelve years old, is standing on the veranda of a large colonial house in Howrah, Shalimar. In the distance, workers are arriving for the early-morning shift at the paint factory, holding stainless-steel tiffin carriers filled with curry and rice. Behind the boy, resting on the wooden slats of the veranda floor is a large trunk and a small suitcase. Inside the inner pocket of the suitcase is a leather-bound passport with a newly fitted photograph inside. The boy notices a few birds scattering from the fortress of tall palm trees which line the Shalimar Botanical Gardens.

The boy is thinking about the word hand-written on the tags of his suitcase: *Darjeeling*. He is old enough to know that he will be very much alone in Darjeeling, but does not appear to be frightened. He is humming, in fact, tying up his shoelaces, smoothing down his hair. He is thinking about the food that his newly appointed gurkha will bring him, a guardian whose presence will be announced through the smell of warm rice and mutton curry, syrupy swirls of *jalebis* fresh from the vendors in the local village.

Inside the house, a couple argue about the fate of this boy. Their voices carry out into the hallway. The boy kicks some dust into the air and shuffles about. At this point, the boy becomes aware of the fact that he is a problem, like an intersection of creases that disturbs the flatness of the starched sheets on the washing line in the garden. His thoughts turn again to the taste of *jalebis.*

A snatched word from inside suddenly rests in the air: 'Dar-jee-ling'.

Many years from now, a young woman has just picked some apples from the orchard in her village in Hampshire, England. She has long black hair and almond-shaped eyes like her great-grandmother's. At home, she slices the apples and turns them in a heavy saucepan, adding cardamom and ginger, tapping the cast-iron pan against the licking flames of a stove. She moves slowly, her thoughts tumbling along with the sound of the dishwasher and the radio, as the edges of the past and the future enter her vision sideways, out of the corner of her eye.

Albury

His eyes are closed in thought. No, his eyes are closed in *feeling*. Or, is it both thought and feeling, that enters his body now? How far can the mind travel when illness is spreading fast across the body? All the way, I wonder, back to Shalimar?

He has stopped listening to music, but he used to enjoy Foster and Allen, or Kenny Rogers. Maybe he heard the whistling wind through the banyan trees in India in the chords of the Country blues, or maybe it was the inherent theme of nostalgia in the lyrics which kept him singing along, bobbing along, head above the water, eyes to the sky, hands reaching forwards, always, past the breakwaters and out of the blue. It was not only my father who enjoyed Country music – a distant aunt had once taken me to a Country music festival in the park near her home in Essex. When we returned to her house, she cooked rice for us in a pressure cooker and gave me scoops of vanilla ice cream. Earlier that day, I had tried on cowboy boots and a fringed leather jacket. I could still smell the leather on my fingers when I put the ice cream to my mouth. The bass notes of the electric guitars rolled into the house through the windows, and I listened to it as I devoured my ice cream in a bowl painted with a Chinese decoration.

I travel home one night from university to our flat in Albury and I hear Dolly Parton's voice on the radio as the bus crosses the road into the hills and the signal dips in and out, causing intermittent breaks in the song. We swerve and swivel through narrow lanes, further and further into the valley and its greenness, dissolving into a starry night as I leave the city behind. I am always the last person to leave the bus and I step off into virtually uninhabited territory, more sheep hugging the land than people wandering through it. Dolly is still singing as I step off the bus. I am not sure if I like this genre of music, but I know that Dolly's lyrics tell me truthful things about self-knowledge and forgiveness. I feel as though I have disembarked from the city and entered my own prairie. There are no horses in these woods, but I hear their hooves approaching along the dirt track, hoops of dust in these frontier lands as I leave my very own wagon behind, the wheels punching out the rhythms in the still of the parkland in Albury.

Often, and only if I am alone, I go on singing in the dark as I walk home from the bus stop. I do this, in part, because I'm a little frightened, but also because it passes the time till I near my destination. My father and I never sang together, though I do know his singing voice, which I recall as tuneful and sombre mainly because I heard it at funerals. My small face looked up at the parted Bible in his hands while I mimed the words.

We never danced together, either. It is one on a long list of things we never did together. I once saw him dancing with my mother on the eve of the Millennium with a green paper hat lopsided on his head and crisps in his open mouth. They spin around the room, posing, and I take a photo. It seems to me, now, that they are like the figures in Pierre-Auguste Renoir's French Impressionist painting 'Dance at Bougival' (*La Danse à Bougival*). Each time I remember this moment, my parents take on an increasing likeness to Renoir's couple, dancing close together, holding hands. My father's green paper hat is replaced with the large straw one that the male dancer famously wears in Renoir's portrait. My mother's jumper is replaced with white folds – the summer dress worn by the girl that Renoir so vividly depicted. Elements of the two images alternate in my mind as they unsettle into each other. As a child, I had meticulously copied this painting as part of a school art project. Perhaps I fill in the blanks of my own memory with other, familiar textures.

On the way up to the flat, I think of my parents dancing together, but now I see them painted as Renoir might have imagined them, brushstrokes visible and feathery, pastel colours, a series of swimming shapes across the room: light spreading over their arms as they seem to turn towards me now. The synthetic, fern-coloured shapes which had once swirled around on our carpet below their feet in the photograph I had taken have now expanded and moved behind their heads, like the blurred foliage which forms part of the backdrop to Renoir's dancers.

I am still singing as I reach the door to our flat. At the edges of my vision, I see coloured movement spread across the skirting boards and the hem of a girl's dress – or was it my mother's? – which I try to cling to.

It has been two months since my father's diagnosis with cancer and we have spent a week at the new flat in Surrey with the little moat which is filled with trout. Our high attic windows frame the clouds and let in perfect squares of light. But they are also entrapping and make it impossible to see any sort of view unless standing on tiptoes: I'm not very tall, so I see even less than my husband out of these windows in the eaves of the old Gothic house. I have nothing to look at, to bind me to the present. Instead, I listen.

It is somewhere between the late afternoon and the evening and I hear pheasants whooping and clucking outside like a broken voice-box stammering on an old fashioned dolly, somewhere between a hiccup and a cry. For a Londoner like me, this noise is disturbing. I think about the incongruity of this sound, the noise of the English countryside which I have had, until now, no knowledge of. There is a distinct who-o-o-oop-whoop, wup-wup-wup call, compounded by the sound of travelling as the birds fly unsteadily, clumsily, in tightly gathered bouts of movement, shuttling past the window. Sitting on the ledge of the window, I see a bird move across the gardens and I hold my breath as it juts forwards, about to step off the grass and into that sloping, diagonal movement. To call this flight would be inaccurate, it is a very awkward propulsion.

About a fifty-minute drive away, my father is dying in our home, awake, listening to the noises outside. He is turning once, twice, in a bed that is broken at the lower half, springs gone. I don't realise this until a visitor points it out to me. My mother is lying on the other side of the bed, asleep with the duvet over her face. In our flat, I look at the pheasants shaking their amber plumage. I start to admit to myself that there is a stone in my chest, just a little beach pebble, turning a fraction sideways. It is the weight of the pebble I am now trying to determine: how can I measure such inner, imminent implosion? What dawns on me is the slow, steady hum of separation from them, my parents and, then, the drift to nothingness, the evaporation of familial connection. I am far away.

There is no clear flow of thought here. My body has become electrified with the feeling of falling, dropping, caught in this state. A pheasant moves across a hedge and stammers towards flight. I shuffle high up on the window ledge of the flat and bring my knees to my chest, tucking my body into the alcove. I have just reached the age of twenty-seven and I can't imagine my future any longer. All is drowned out by the sound of the pebble turning and the clock on the side of the wall which vibrates each time a person marches past the corridor outside our flat.

The moment you know someone is dying, and dies *across* time and space while you are sat in your new home, is the most awful kind of limbo and liminal time. Your whole head is in the mouth of a tiger. Death tumbles out of everywhere, like sand in your shoe. Judith Kerr's much-loved children's story, *The Tiger Who Came to Tea* is well known for its allusions to Kerr's experiences of the Second World War; the tiger's hunger and thirst seen as a metaphor for the destructive forces of human warfare. But, the tiger is also death. Here, quiet and, seemingly, polite in his request to be invited into Sophie's family home. Like the tiger's hunger, which cannot be satiated until all is incorporated, consumed, emptied, thoughts of death are consuming me whole.

Unexpectedly, a story of another deadly animal greets me here, in the dark, curdling with the image of a tiger as I sit and wait for news about my father. Once, my maternal grandparents noticed a leak during heavy rainfall and its plink-plonk song beat down on their veranda. Insistent as she was, Phyllis, my grandmother, asked my grandfather, Lewis, to investigate and so he went, trudging out into the rain. At first, he sees nothing but the colour of the charcoal-grey pipe, then, a heavier patchwork of straw-coloured shapes and loose, stretched, octagonal blacks. The rain whips his face so he is looking through sheets of movement, rain and pipework, water and plastic guttering. He reaches for the pipework in order to inspect its insides. But there are no clogged leaves or moss. Yet, something gleams: a living oil painting the shape of a log. This part of the pipe, surely, shines *too* brightly against the guttering and calls attention to itself because it is a river and a log, liquid and solid all at once. Was it soil? Why, then, so beautifully patterned? Here, at my grandfather's fingertips, comes the moment of realisation which stakes his body, his legs, to the ground. Lewis Benjamin Duncan is a soldier in the British army, of Scottish and Burmese descent, and he has learned to recognise fear and quell its spread. Still, he remained pinned to the ground. Far from the Irrawaddy River, a fifteen-foot Burmese python has entered the suburbs in Rangoon and attached itself to my maternal grandparents' exterior pipework at their home. Mistaking its body for a drainpipe, Lewis had felt the python's moving scales. For years to come, he remembered its unending, sliding shape.

Lewis was not swallowed whole by the Burmese python, though the largest of these species are well known to have that capacity, and after this moment he goes on to live for almost another forty years before he passes away in his 80s at St Helier Hospital, Surrey. Along with his passing, I witnessed many other close relatives dying in hospital before my sixteenth birthday: the simple fact being that I was born late and everyone was already old. My father was 44 years old by the time I came along. By my mid-thirties I count ten deaths: both grandmothers (old age, pneumonia), a grandfather, two twenty-something cousins (a motorcycling accident and death by misadventure), an uncle (old age, cancer), an uncle (brain tumour), a distant aunt (old age), my father (cancer), my father's sister (old age, a heart condition). Bobby, a black lab crossed with a Doberman, died shortly after my aunt's husband, Hugh. *Remember in Burma, we say when the dog dies there will be no more deaths*, whispers my aunt to my mother in the kitchen. My mother says nothing. I imagine her remembering when she accidentally cut short the life of a canary perched atop a door and did not tell my father. SLAM. *What does the death of a canary foretell?*

In Albury, I dress quickly and take our dog out. I walk straight out of the doors of our flat, down the steps and into the road. There are narrow country lanes and I do not know which way to turn. I go left. Left feels right. Our dog is small, a Yorkshire terrier, so I put his lead on and get ready to pick him up if we travel too far for his short legs. I walk north of the flat and I am wearing blue leather boots with embroidered details on the ankles, a folk pattern. The woodland park is a long, slow drop until you reach the old iron gates at the foot of the hill. It seems I am the only walker on this path, but it is a clear day and I am feeling optimistic. I decide to follow the road, walking side by side with the traffic, and make my way over to Guildford. The city is a good twenty-minute drive away, but I am taking the longer route, by foot, so I calculate a few hours' walk.

This is when I begin walking. I had never walked far before. I am a city child. The furthest we would walk was to my secondary school, ten minutes away, or along the Uxbridge road, right to the very end before you reached Uxbridge. You could buy sweets from a department store there and a shop sold cake mix and dry goods by the kilo. Walking was never leisurely, it was practical, necessary because my mother didn't drive and I needed to get to school. If it rained, I questioned the need to go in, I was afraid of the way my black hair would frizz in the rain and mushroom, altering my fringe and turning everything wavy. Like most of my school friends at the time, we all wanted perfectly straight hair, the kind you see in teen magazines with models whose faces rarely reflected our own.

I discovered that walking partially dissolved the pebble which had made its home in my chest. It was a salve, of course. Our little frayed-at-the-edges dog tottered beside me and I pounded onwards through foliage, woodland, deserted roads, treading over faded crisp packets and sweet wrappers. Earlier in the week I had stood on the Strand outside the entrance to King's College, London, and told a kind friend I had such a pain in my chest that I couldn't concentrate on anything. The London buses passed us and we stood under the shelter of the college buildings. She said: 'You need to cry, you are holding it in.' What was the 'it'? I wondered: there was not one singular thing, but pluralities of devastation.

The thing is, I could not cry and so I walked instead. I went home that night, walking from the bus stop, suddenly aware of my own body and the physical problem I had with grief, because it was grief, and I was frequently, more often than not, holding my breath.

Out of the door and now decidedly walking, on a walk, on a jaunt, or whatever you wish to call it, I realised I had never traversed this far before with my own feet because where I grew up it was probably unwise or unsafe. It would be foolish to walk for hours through unknown territory. It was a sweet feeling, passing the lush green hills and the horizon filled with the silhouettes of black oaks (*Quercus velutina*) and lime trees. I passed a petrol garage and bought a can of Coke. The dog sat on a curb with me, visibly tired. This was a lunar landscape, to me, another world, and I felt as far away from home as possible. The constant movement through this new place seemed, conversely, to ground me. I was navigating a new sense of home and I was like the starlings or the hawks which I would see skim the trees.

Watching all the birds along the B roads in Surrey, in the quiet afternoon light, I see my father holding one of his canaries on the tip of his finger. He says, 'Just stroke its head, gentle, watch the colour of its feathers.' How fragile they would feel on my fingertips. 'You have to stay very still,' my father says. We had kept dozens as a child. Later, we would collect the dead young which had fallen from white plastic nests in the corners of their aviary, powdery feathers falling slowly from their perches. The air smelled of canary seed, bittersweet. It was my mother and not my father who would go around the aviary with a big black bin liner, collecting the fallen young, indifferent, as I stood in her aproned shadow. My mother's voice says, '*saype*'. I'm not sure if she says this word to herself, or to me. I just know the word, but she never tells me what it means. Over time, as I hear this word more and more in the mouths of my mother and my aunt, I learn that is it their way of speaking about the dead, a subject which requires the Burmese parts of themselves to name it, as if the employment of all the English words applicable here would be an act of injustice. *Saype*, they say, with such tenderness that it sits abjectly within a sentence full of hard English vowels and consonants. For a long time, I find it hard to recognise my mother's voice when she speaks like this, it takes years for it to become what it is: I have to accept all the parts of her, and of myself, one by one. These words and their sounds remain with me long after I have left my mother behind in Hayes.

We walked for another few miles and down a dark track filled with beech trees. We reached Newlands Corner, the famous site where Agatha Christie's car was discovered when she went missing in the 1920s. Crossing the road and then down another A road, I discovered a restaurant which had opened in the woods and I peered in through the windows. A small lightbox with a menu taped to it was fitted outside. It was covered in dead moths. I wondered why no one had changed the menu, or removed the moths. There were lacy wings folded into other dead insects and specks of black matter where the moths had disintegrated, trapped in the lightbox. Rorschach blots. The wording of Italian gastronomy, now very unappealing, lingering underneath the wing-strewn piece of yellowing paper.

At one point, I miss my footing and slip into a ditch near the roadside. The dog ambles forwards and I grip the soil half-covered in grass. A grass stain on my dress and up my thigh. A bruise. My heart pounds deeply for a moment. I laugh to myself, staring at the aquamarine boots with their two-inch platform heels. Standing up, I take the dog lead in my left hand and avoid another oncoming car. I refuse to feel lost. I do not give in to that sensation. *Don't say anything*, I think. Better not say I was nearly run over on an A road in Surrey.

My father was once asked to attend a work 'do' in Farnham and he found himself lost for over an hour. He always hated driving and would breathe heavily, slowly at the wheel, smoking Old Holborn roll ups and using the ashtray intermittently. The air would be marked by a stale gash of tobacco and crumbling ash. The driver's window wound down. He had no sense of orientation. It was not about the possession of a map, but rather the feeling of the unknown. He had crossed oceans and travelled to England by boat, yet he feared distance, moving only within the boundaries of home, my aunt's house in Ealing, my grandmother's house in Surrey, my school in Hayes. After years of house arrest under the ruling of the Japanese, both my father and my aunt would seem to be happiest at home, unwilling to adventure far beyond, residual traces of their arrest surfacing as possible agoraphobia or maybe, simply, a desperate need to be safely inside one's home. In our homes, we become accustomed to a familiar air.

In her book *The Forgetting of Air*, the philosopher Luce Irigaray writes about how we have forgotten about the air that surrounds us and how we should try to live together with respect for this space, or what she describes as a particular place of mutual being. What kind of air exists between us, now? I think of the clichés of country 'air' and city smog, the suffocation of the city, its miasma of dust and toxic exhaust fumes, and the perceived freedoms and health benefits of rural habitation. Right now, I can only feel the hard pebble in my chest growing. I grew up underneath the flight paths of Heathrow Airport, even working there for a time at WHSmith while I took my 'A' Levels, and we lived on a main road filled with traffic more or less until I reached adulthood. When we left I was supposed to shout victoriously from the back of a car like Muriel in P. J. Hogan's film *Muriel's Wedding* as she leaves her small home town behind. Instead, we piled into a friend's silver Skoda with our belongings thrown into the boot, knowing we would be back to nurse my father in the half-term holidays.

Still walking in my platform boots, I reach Guildford at around 4 p.m. I approach the top end of the high street and suddenly all the shops and the crowds of people come into view. The light is fading and I realise I have spent the day walking. It is beyond unusual for me. It is a triumph. On the way home, in the car, I look out at the sliding landscape and the route I had taken all day to traverse. I don't say anything about my slip into the road. I can hear the birds in the forest. The sun passes through the branches of the silver birches like a blessing. At night, I do not hear the pheasants and we close our door, but sometimes someone walks past in the hallway and the thin walls momentarily betray their presence. Then the phone rings out in the dark. It is the hospital.

Pigeon's blood

Rosehip, wound about the bone, Tigermoth butterfly, papillon sunset, clasp against pulse, reflection in the pool of water by the hawthorn, and the briar. Light lozenge, light lozenge, it casts a rainbow over a book in my hands, or over the stove when I cook rice in a pan, olive, amber and lavender but crimson, too, cut the bright slivers and still, its golden weight. Jewels, she gave me. Its companion is pure, and almost weightless, two Indian sovereigns hammered as thin as two blades of grass, a chorus. Between these, a chasm of time, drawn deep from the flint and rocks, strange geologies, sediment, sentiments, a geography and the song it never sang to me. I have never seen an Indian sunset and I have never seen a Burmese lake. On my wrists, hillsides reflected in their nets of light. A double-dart, swoop, no, a loop, a binding. A dark spell. My grandmother and my aunt give me these blessings in their alchemical forms, gemstone and gold. Matter and mineral, histories stolen and reclaimed in their presence, all along the light lozenge links in time, linking in time.

These gemstones, inherited jewels, finally arrived in my hands at the age of only nine years old.

It is the summer and we are celebrating my birthday. All the women in my family are gathered around an extendable wooden table in our conservatory playing Pontoon, a very old-fashioned kind of Black Jack card game.

I watch her hands effortlessly split a deck of cards.

Phyllis, my maternal grandmother, is counting very slowly. This has the overall effect of sounding as though she has hypnotised someone with a silver stopwatch and is calling them back into the present, one number at a time, '2, 4, 5...' Her voice rolls the vowels, accented and clipping at the consonants in the way that calls to mind the distinctive voice of the Indian actress and cookery writer Madhur Jaffrey. I had seen Jaffrey's television programmes as a child and immediately connected her to my 'nanny': they belonged to the same generation and both were daughters of Colonial India but, most of all, they sounded almost identical. 'Fetch me a plate child, don't hand me those samosas like that,' she says. She calls me, 'Divina', or the name gets stuck somehow and morphs into half of another name, my uncle's name, David: 'Divi...Davi... Davina...' Years later, I hear Jaffrey on Radio 4 and I turn to face her, instinctively turning my body towards the little blue radio on our kitchen worktop. Nanny was speaking to us in our kitchen.

With a ruffle of her dyed brown curls at the nape of her neck, she goes back to counting the cards on the table. My father's sister, Adelaide, is at the other end of the table sipping sherry, crinkling her lips into an oblong 'O', as she turns her cards over. My grandmother's gold bracelets shiver and clink on her wrists. I can still hear them now. These bracelets were fashioned from a few rare Indian sovereign coins, liquid capital, and a memento made of Indian gold before they left for England. Everywhere she goes, I hear the bangles ringing, dropping over her arms and stopping at her elbows when she scratches her chin, moves a hair from her face or separates the cards when she plays Pontoon.

At the table, all the women are speaking in a patchwork of Punjabi, English, Burmese; for the nine-year-old at the table this is, really, a study of adult behaviour as all interact in a way that summons the Indian summers of my own mother's childhood, the pool parties and drinks on the veranda. They have transported themselves to another temporal zone under the single-glazed windows of our conservatory in Hayes and the table is a conduit for memory, the cards are conversations folding and collapsing in time. I am close by, near enough to see the strands of my aunt's dark, permed hair and catch the scent of her hands, washed with lemons. I can see the split trace of her lipstick on a glass of sweet sherry. Closer, my chin rests on her shoulder, my nose inhabiting the space near the line of pearls at her neck, breathing in her hair and hiding, perched on an occasional chair.

There is a silence as the cards are dealt. A pause. But I am not watching the cards. I am looking at their faces. My grandmother's long earlobes, my aunt's rouged cheeks. My aunt is the Queen of Hearts from Lewis Carroll's *Alice in Wonderland*, fierce and red-lipped, rosy-cheeked, ready to send heads rolling; my grandmother is a laughing Joker, bending the edges of her cards and tapping the pine table. Sometimes she sings. These two 'rhythms' of behaviour sit incongruously in the air and I pluck at their awkwardness like invisible strings on an oddly shaped instrument. A bird lands on the wooden bird table on our lawn and my father scatters rice, waving from the garden. My aunt purses her lips in frustration because my grandmother has just mistaken her glass for her own. I can see my Uncle Hugh outside with my father as he smokes an Old Holborn roll up. They are walking down the line of roses planted along the fence, my father's head bowed, listening as if he has heard a prayer. My half-sister from my mother's first marriage is also at the table, twenty-one years my senior.

My grandmother continues to sip from the glass that is not hers and my aunt sighs deeply. In truth, there was a subtle history of unspoken tension between these two sides of my family, which followed them to England. Both families had known each other in India and Burma, but they were very different, one family conservative and restrained, my father's side, and the other, party-goers and highly social, my mother's. These differences would manifest themselves at family gatherings, never openly admitted, but there in the way they interacted with each other. Everyone would be measuring each other's behaviour.

My aunt always referred to those who did not conform to the stiff-upper-lipped image of 'Englishness' as 'Anglo-banglo': too unrefined, flaunting their indigenous ethnicity and not fully embracing the Colonial identity my father's family had tended to subscribe to, thus making their own mixed heritage 'palatable'. Yet, everyone was performing in an 'Anglo-banglo' way at the table when we played cards; everyone was free to drop the on-going act which was the correct performance of Colonialism. My aunt would whisper in Burmese and my mother would laugh loudly, repeating phrases I never understood, but knew were connected to an intimate knowledge of what it felt like to be a woman in my family. Where was I in this political scenario? *Who* was I? I just wanted to feel the warmth of their company and never wanted it to end.

Despite their differences, and after many years in England together, my father's sister and my mother's mother loved each other and shared many Christmas Days and birthdays in my family home. Most likely from either Goa or Kerala, Phyllis was a ukulele player, a singer and a dancer. She carried with her a black Spanish fan with a white lace trim and she wore Oil of Ulay face cream, Max Factor face powder and Boots No. 7 lipstick every day of her life. She was a Catholic and always wore a St Christopher pendant, patron saint of travellers. A few years off 90 and struggling with Parkinson's, Phyllis sang her heart out during her last Christmas, slightly out of tune but enjoying herself nevertheless, as she accompanied my then fiancé on the trombone. That Christmas, I wore a black Chinese dress and she told me I looked like 'Lily', her brother's wife. She crooned and my father smiled as she moved her fingers in the air, the gold bangles dropping down further now, past her elbows and along her upper arms which poke out of the folds of her cardigan. She passed away a year before I was married. My aunt was at the funeral and sat quietly dressed in black and holding my mother's hand, genuinely lost for words.

In the summer, Phyllis would pull a large tartan shopper in and out of various spice stores in Southall and load it full of packets of saffron, nuts, rice and tinned bamboo, taking this precious haul back to Carshalton in Surrey as if it had come all the way from India itself. She still enjoyed speaking in Punjabi and when we were not playing card games she was teaching me to count: *ikk, do, tinn, chaar, panj, chhe, satt, ath, naun, das, giaran, baran, teran, chaudan, pandran.* I have never forgotten these lessons. Her husband would accompany my father to the bookies, tweed cap on his head and a newspaper tucked under his arm. Were they counting in English, Punjabi or Burmese, as they placed their bets?

Sat sri akaal. Mera naan haga Davina.

('Hello. My name is Davina.')

For shopping: *Aa Kinney da haga?*

('What is the price?')

For politeness: *Shukriya.*

('Thank you'.)

When they were not visiting us, we would visit them at Easter. We would make the journey to see my maternal grandparents in Surrey, stopping along the way to pick up onion bhajis and samosas wrapped in the proverbial 'beggars parchment' brown paper. There would also be *rasagullas* in syrup, a kind of cardamom doughnut without the hole, pistachio and coconut *barfi*, all cherry-picked from Babu Tandoori Restaurant in Southall, whipping the car into a tiny space on a side-road before entering this mirrored bazaar. I often saw containers of Chana beef curry in the little snack bar at the foyer; my most vivid memory of it was in Babu, lined up with several other curries in rectangular aluminium trays, all thick, varying shades of brown and red, streaked with yoghurt, the little mounds of meat islanded in a pool of coloured viscous gravy. It was awkward for me to look at these things in the trays: they were neither entirely familiar, nor foreign, and this rendered them acutely abject.

We shared the food and my grandmother's golden bangles swayed over the packets of spices, their subtle song never leaving me. Years later, I held the gold bracelets in my hands and felt their weight like a swallows' nest in my palm. She was gone, but her fingers were still caressing the air, reaching for the high notes.

While my maternal grandmother liked to go shopping, my father's sister, my aunt Adelaide, liked to cook. On my birthday, she brings over a tray of Sanwin Makin, her Burmese version of banana fudge. Between mouthfuls my utterances make the sounds 'sinna-ma-kane', and this becomes the first Burmese word I ever speak.

My mispronunciation is typical. I would misname the foods we ate, clumsily trying to mimic the Burmese dialect, making new words which only made sense to me. Here and there, I picked up other Burmese words, often creeping into English sentences. As a toddler, my rather audacious aunt taught me how to curse in Burmese and it became a retort which I would shout back at her in the passenger seat of my uncle's car as they drove away from our home. As I called out, I would raise my arms high above my head and make a movement, palm to palm, a gesture, a little joke we shared between us. Your hands must be slapped together as you speak, one hand sliding over the fingers of another. This is the Burmese way of expressing an expletive. My father would laugh, slightly sheepishly, as he carried me back inside our house. Though a little blunt and inappropriate, it was a lesson, really: in her own way, she was teaching me to be armoured, to be fierce.

Back in the summer of 1946, my nineteen-year-old aunt slips out of an open window and joins a party. Her mother forbade her from going out at night, so she waits until she can hear the dinner things being put away and the wireless downstairs before she pulls a *crepe de chine* dress over her head and carries patent-leather party shoes in a bag around her neck. She likes brooches so she wears one of those, too. Admittedly, it is far too late in the evening, but she remains determined. Luckily for her, the height of the building is not the problem here because she lives in a bungalow. It is her father's sleeping sheep dogs, seven of them, which are the main worry. Her youngest brother is also sleeping with one of the dogs, Mabel, on his bed, in the other room beside her own. She pulls open a window and leaps up on to the ledge. She faces the darkness of the garden now. Soon, she is running fast along the grass, her left hand carrying a black scarf. She takes this risk because she cannot sleep and while her head is clear during the day, it is the night which carries the unwanted things into her room. The war is now over in Burma yet she keeps recalling the hands of men, digging the soil in the forests, deeper and deeper they dig. She witnessed nothing, but when the men return, if they return, she sees their hands, shaking still, because the work is unending and it will never stop until the war does. They fade further, each day, into papery cut-outs, as they part with pieces of themselves, their bodies sacrificed to what seemed like an insatiable creature dwelling in the trees: a wolf she has no name for. Her mother will not acknowledge the sadness in her eyes. Mostly, they cannot look at each other (though that will change in time). So, now she cares only for the present and the party she most desires to attend. She meets a young engineering graduate of Rangoon University at this party and, within two years she will be married. Then, they will travel far away from the wolf in the forests in Burma. He tells her he has already bought a house in Shalimar in the Howrah District of West Bengal.

I arrive when she is retired and has lived in England for over twenty-five years. With her own children all grown up and no grandchildren as yet, I surprise everyone – a new baby in the family. This woman who was forbidden to wear lipstick on her wedding day, or proper fitting undergarments, teaches me expletives, how to be improper, because propriety became less important as she aged. With me, she shared the secret of her mischievous nature, suppressed by the Edwardian values of parents and, perhaps, their over-protectiveness following the war. Together, we fashion a lexicon of unspoken words, exiled sounds, if you will, which only we know and share. When loved ones die, this is what we lose, not the things we said to each other but the ghosts of the things which encircled language, the spaces of contact in between the words. Here, too, language is in exile. Language is adrift and loosened from the three sandbanks of country, continent and nationhood.

At the wrists, 4711 eau de cologne and, occasionally, Samsara. Mottled red, uneven folds of an M&S cardigan skim her figure, the line of her buttons softly altered after breast cancer, but nevertheless abundant and strong. In my twenties, I watch her ever more closely. My elderly aunt Adelaide is full of smiles, but also unexpected wit and joyful laughter, like a schoolgirl, as calculated, often under-the-belt retorts leave her lips. As a teenager, I do not hold anyone's hand, not even my own mother's, but I will hold hers. I press my fingers around the soft flesh of her palm. Wide, gesturing hands like mine.

We have all visited her in her home in Ealing, passing down the corridor as the lights flicker on, fingers skimming the raised surfaces of its flocked wallpaper and swirling brown and yellow carpets. It smells of Dettol and freshly cut lemons (ones she uses to cleanse her hands and worktops after she has made a stew or a curry). She was born in Rangoon (Yangon), but lives in this tomb now, housebound and frozen in time, with the same décor she and her late husband chose at least fifty years ago. The only new addition to this cocoon, this enveloping shrine to the past and every moment ever lived in this house, is a chestnut-coloured chesterfield sofa, bought just before her husband died from throat cancer (perhaps caused by toxic fumes from the paint company he worked for in Shalimar, or was it the DDT from the insecticide he sprayed in their garden?) My father brought him bottled mineral water. He was so thirsty all of the time. His ghost lives at the front of the house, enfolded into the wallpaper and the shape of the rectangular single-glazed bay window half-dressed in nets. An Anglo-Italian born in Burma, my uncle never raised his voice and he listened with his head bowed, gentle and whispering to my aunt. He never called her by her name, he called her 'girl'. She called him 'Hughie'.

The chesterfield is wiped religiously with a leather cloth and no one ever sits on it: it is a solid, gleaming shrine to her beloved, locked away in the room no one ever visits at the front of the house. She lives in the kitchen, now full of damp and shaky kitchen units. She looms over large pans of boiling rice and spiced meats, huffing as she tilts them over the sink in order to strain away the extra water or steady them over the dish stand. She will never replace this wonky kitchen because she knows every corner of it, like the house itself. Then, gradually, she starts to struggle with the labour involved in making her own food every day, in walking up the steep Edwardian staircase to her bedroom, or the walk from the long hallway to the front door (she sits in her chair at the back of the house while we let ourselves out and post the key, once we've locked up, back through the letterbox). As we leave, I remind myself she won't be here forever, but how can that be true?

Once, during the final year of my undergraduate studies, we gathered outside on the avenue and made a little film, using her home as our set. We filmed throughout March, arriving daily, and the cherry blossom from the trees fell like pink waves of confetti onto our equipment. My aunt stayed inside making tea and frying bacon when we arrived at 8 a.m. She greeted everyone with a blanket around her shoulders; she was a clever woman and her impish wit and sarcasm cut through the sense of unfamiliarity and early-morning starts. Standing in the hallway, my aunt welcomed cameras and lighting rigs, huge metal boxes with lenses and tripods piled high against the golden, gaudily embossed wallpaper (the same wallpaper a cousin had scraped and peeled as a toddler).

Early every Monday, my father and mother take my aunt to the supermarket and this steady rhythm of shopping and sharing tea becomes a ritual over more than a decade after my uncle's death. After shopping, my father would stand outside on the parched lawn behind the Edwardian semi, rolling up cigarettes and watching the skies. There was great comfort in this routine, and the resolute intimacy of resilience and kindness. We would sit in her kitchen underneath a gilt-framed replica of John Constable's *The Hay Wain* and I would glance up at the figures in the pastoral ode to farming life, contemplating the softness of the horse's mane and the gentle slope of the farm hand's back on the wooden wagon as he made his way across the River Stour in Suffolk.

On the other side of the room, above the chimney breast, was an oil painting of a still life, fruit gleaming in a bronze bowl. Beneath this, two shire horses in porcelain. These, too, reminded me of my father, a great lover of horses. I remember the weight in my hands of two bronze ponies, heavy enough to break glass or bones, that lived carefully positioned on a shelf in our living room. Animal life existed in this form throughout my childhood, with the exception of my father's canaries or a few pet dogs along the way – animal life was decorous and deeply connected to a sense of taste, of class and of appreciation for things which didn't really figure in our lives, but maybe once represented some sense of home. Of course, my father used to ride horses in India.

Now, Adelaide is a thin echo, gone just before my second child arrives, so I imagine her inside the house with my uncle, gone years before. Her face and body at the kitchen table flickers in my memory like one of those holograms in a science fiction film – there, and not there. I don't know anymore. When was the last time I saw her? Of course, the answer is 'every day'. Every day I see her face, every day I think of her. When I am tired and worried, I can see her at the end of the bed, or at the window, pursing her lips together. 'Don't worry about all of that rubbish,' she says. Then, a child skips past a door, or the phone rings, and the room is emptied again of her presence.

I cling to these images of my aunt in her kitchen like Mikage, the young woman in Banana Yoshimoto's *Kitchen*. Mourning the loss of her grandmother, Mikage drags her bed into the kitchen and sleeps next to the soothing hum of her refrigerator. I want to put my hands on my aunt's linen tablecloth and listen to the sound of her clock above the pulley of the old Edwardian clothes airer which hung from the ceiling. She was always there when I got off the bus and made an impromptu visit, she was always there on the end of the telephone; if I stand on the threshold to her house long enough, surely she will come out of the porch and open the door. Surely she will say, 'Come, come, what do you want to eat?' Even if you pull a tree out of the ground, its roots will have threaded through the other trees around it and it will go on providing a scaffolding to the living systems it has dwelled within for years to come.

Back in our conservatory on my ninth birthday, my aunt's husband calls out from the other side of the room. My aunt takes out an extra strong mint from her handbag and answers her husband without taking her eyes off the cards being dealt to her. My aunt is drinking little sips of sherry. Every time she takes a sip, the tip of her tongue touches the top of the glass. She shuffles in her seat, spreading her hand of cards into a fan. I peek over her shoulder, thinking about dinner and leftovers from the party: ham covered in foil and cookies in a tin with a navy blue and white Wedgewood print. My father has let our canary out of her birdcage and her yellow feathers dance across the ceiling. His finger is held out and she hops on. 'Your father thinks that thing is a racing pigeon,' my aunt says. I do not really know what she means. *How do you race a pigeon? How does it know how to return home?*

A few days later, my aunt opens her cupboards in her bedroom and, instead of a Christmas present, which I greedily expect, she passes me a small blue velvet jewellery bag. Inside is an art nouveau bracelet with twelve semi-precious stones, and some 'pigeon's blood' rubies (the Burmese name for these jewels), cut into rectangular lozenges and set in gold. She tells me it belonged to her maternal grandmother, Parquala, who was from Mogok in Myanmar's Shan state.

My aunt fastens Parquala's bracelet on to my wrists and I hear the clasp click into place. Her hands make the shape of the Burmese curse she had taught me. She says, with one finger pointing in front of the closed lips of her mouth, 'shhh'.

Cloch na Blarnan

Enchantment is vulnerable. Vulnerability is enchantment.
Enchantment, like vulnerability, is necessary.

SO MAYER, FROM 'THE UNBROKEN'

Still. A tangled word on her tongue. Breath against the
flatness. Drifts of wind settle into the stone. The taste of
silver salt on her lips. The caulk and the limestone. On her
back, her whole body is a cascade of hair and cloth. Her
face descends into the gaps in the stone. Here, the world is
the sky, the fixing of her gaze on a solid wall which is also a
rockface, a parapet, a veil. She closes her eyes.

Iron railings between her fingers, she leans into the stones.
Too close, and she will bruise her face, scratch her forehead.
The iron spins ice through her fingernails and the joints in
her arms, the same arms which held on to the handles of large
cooking pots and lifted her children from the jetty and out
on to the steamer boats in India. Her palms, tight around the
railings, once felt the rolling weight of a pestle and mortar as
she ground cumin and mustard seeds, now slipping, faltering.

Feet are tucked underneath, toes curled. Her shoes are
black patent leather. She never wears trainers. A rush of
blood to the head. Someone, just behind her, asks her to
stop. 'No, you'll fall, come back', but she is still bent under
the rock. The sun passes behind the corner of the parapet
and blinds her, momentarily. To stop now would be foolish.
She has walked all day. Why stop when you are already here,
at this point? She has a tear in her tan-coloured tights and
the oval shape gapes open like a parting of wings.

Her eyes settle on a tiny, dark shape in the wall. A dead
beetle on the rocks. Remnants of a life. She is careful not to
get too close. She slides sideways.

Does the rock smell sweet? Or, is it her daughter's perfume hanging in the air, gardenia and roses.

Her mouth parts. Her mouth is the shape of a rhyme, like my father's mouth opening as he ate the forbidden mangoes in India. Her son's trespass. Now the fruit is a rock, her skin against its brittle surface. Her skin against the rocks, the rocks against the sky. She has travelled hundreds of miles and her body carries the weight of time and space as she continues to bend backwards and prepares to press her lips against this weighted frame, this measure of being, this ancient rock, this great, immense boulder wrought of calcite, or aragonite and dust, this stone they call the Blarney.

Such movement is, of course, sealed with a kiss. All geographical points and orientations, coordinates and place names are unsettled and exhaled through my grandmother's body, a woman in her late 50s standing in Cork, Ireland, kissing the Blarney Stone at a castle under whose battlements one must be lowered in order to deliver a kiss which will bequeath the gift of eloquence or 'the gift of the gab'. Her kiss is elemental, it embodies all of our family history, all of time made flesh, and all of the generations before her.

It was my great-great paternal grandparents, Michael and Johanna Quinlivan, who arrived from Kilrush, Clare. In a letter from the Commonwealth Relations Office at King Charles Street, Whitehall, sent to my grandparents in Burma to confirm my grandfather's British status after the Second World War, Michael was declared a Limerick soldier. He was enlisted by the British East India Company's Madras army on August 19, 1840, a Gunner with the 2nd Battalion Artillery at the age of twenty-two, bound for India on a ship called the *Reliance*. This ship set sail only twice in its lifetime, once in 1840 and once in 1837. I know all of this because my father had collected a handful of records in a sealed plastic wallet and when he died I emptied these out on to his bed, seeing for the first time his birth certificate, along with his passport and fragments of official documents which told the tale of migration, from Ireland to India, from India to England. Somewhere in between all of this was Shalimar and Rangoon. Details are typed out on yellowing paper, names sometimes misspelt or dates slightly incorrect. There were no digital records back then, no archive which would erase such irregularities.

Mysteriously, Michael's wife, Johanna, disappears in my father's records, but is replaced with a 'Georgiana' whose name appears, also, as his wife and mother to Henry, finally, the first generation of Quinlivans to be born in 1869, followed by Richard, my grandfather. His wife, Maggie, visited Ireland soon after her husband's death in Ealing, London. In mourning, she was compelled to kiss the famous stone.

It is a perverse embrace between rock and woman, a tussle, a strange dance. In many ways, it is an echo, or an inversion, of the embrace between the life-sized tiger and the European soldier which is performed through the semi-automaton known as *Tippoo's Tiger*, the object famously held within the Victoria and Albert Museum. Tipu was the sultan of Mysore, India, in the late eighteenth century, and it was with an intense ferocity that he resisted attacks from the British East India Company as they plundered his ancient Kingdom. *Tippoo's Tiger* is an object of vast scale, a supersized toy, which is not actually a toy at all, but a symbol of power. It was made for Sultan Tipu and its principal point of fascination is its ability to produce not only movement, but sound.

Concealed inside the tiger's body is an organ which can be played by moving the dying man's arms, imitating his groans of pain. A kiss, as this object tells us, can also be deadly, but as the air pushes up through its organ, this low, brassy noise becomes the sound of the British Empire collapsing, its lungs filling and contracting for the last time. My grandmother stood at the

Blarney Stone and wished, perhaps, for redemption, the gift that she herself embodied because she stood, teetering, on the fault lines, as all diasporic children do.

Was she thinking of her husband as she kissed the stone? What is the register of this kiss, then? It cannot be tender because the pledge to turn one's body backwards, arched and taut, ribs skywards as if gripped by an invisible belt, is improper, unnatural, uncompromising. It is halfway between a somersault and a handstand. It is a sacrifice, this kiss, a promise, a pact with gravity and a disorientation of the natural laws of the Earth, worthy of the most powerful spells. And, so it is: an offering.

Her lips cannot kiss the rock. It is a blunt relic. She is a living survivor of the atrocities of war and she does not have to do anything anymore unless she desires to. Why kiss this, anyway? This is not her land, nor home, she owes it nothing. She has already given herself whole, once imprisoned by the Japanese and witness to hundreds of war crimes. A kiss of gratitude? A kiss of faithfulness. But, no, it is not that kind of kiss. She decides she has come only for the gift of eloquence it harbours deep within its geology. She is a small half-Burmese, half-German woman with a band of gemstones from her mother's home in Mogok around her wrists; she wishes for an eloquence of language which is complicated here, because she speaks so many all at once.

This is not a kiss, it is an 'ism', or an 'is', no, an 'issss', a meta-mor-pho-sis.

Her face is up close to the rock, nose to nose. Her lips are dry, wind-whipped, cold. Her cheekbones form the features of her Burmese face so they rest a little closer, higher, already, to the stone. Her mouth and the skin around her face brush the surface of the thing which is now all she can see, all she can taste. And then she lets her arms go and the sinewy strands of her upper arms bounce backwards. Her fingertips are on fire.

Buds unfurl at her fingers and whole branches are brought forth. A green spruce aphid (*Elatobium abietinum*) appears at her feet. Leaves accumulate in constellations above her head and the branches keep shooting from her palms. In the air, a sprouting. A blossom. Another. And then another. A living network of winding branches singing their own song from the stone parapet. She is a tree, a teak tree (*Tectona grandis*), like the ones she had seen in Burma. Sapwood and heartwood spun around a kiss. She is laughing. A rush of blood to her head. She has become the spell, the promise of eloquence. At the top of the tree, the emotionless faces of the Buddhist monks from her home in Syriam clasp their hands together and whisper.

My grandmother, Maggie, visited the Blarney Stone at Blarney Castle in Cork, Ireland, but the irony is that I never heard her speak. She had a severe stroke which left her almost entirely without the capacity for speech when I was very small. She was also wheelchair-bound after that and until her death in the early 90s. Her daughter and her son-in-law made a sacrifice, they decided to care for her full-time in the spare room of their home in Ealing, which had always been her home anyway, and so their retirement became a working life, all over again. They took it in their stride and they never complained, though that is not to say that they did not argue with Maggie. She could be difficult and, of course, felt the frustration of the loss of speech and mobility. When family members would visit and recount stories from India and Burma, she would nod slowly and with such comprehension and recognition that even I could grasp them, despite being so little. Her entire face altered. I tried to make her write once, but all she could produce were scraggly lines with a biro, not a single legible word.

The only memory I have of Maggie's voice was during my very early years when she would babysit and find me in our back garden talking to our young neighbour, Wesley, a child of around five or six, a few years older than myself, whose diehard wish, at least in her mind, was to kill me. She imagined he would poison me with dirty water left for his pet tortoise, or cut off my feet when he wielded a garden shovel across my shoes from under the gaps in our fence. This, he very nearly achieved, shoving the metal across the soil like a guillotine. Once he had escaped into our garden and she chased him away, his voice shouting at her as he clambered back over the boundary. I was fascinated by Wesley, despite his violent tendencies. He was a good kid, but he suffered terribly from hyperactivity. I know this because he was not permitted Smarties or coloured sweets of any kind owing to their very high concentration in E numbers; like psychotropic mushrooms, they were believed to send him into a frenetic mania. My grandmother despised him.

To this day, I do not know my own grandmother's voice. I know only the strained sounds she made as she tried to call out for her daughter. She would pull me up close and kiss me, as she kissed the Blarney. She would hide sweet wrappers in the sides of her wheelchair and crisp packets in the holes beside the wheels. She was transfixed by boxing matches on the television, her eyes concentrating on the throwing of punches and the upper cuts. I would comb her thin, silver hair and she would smile at me. I would also steal her special diabetic chocolate from Boots and take whatever was left in the silver tin of pear drops she kept in a drawer by her bed. She was an extremely strong-willed woman and it only took one call out to my aunt for her to run up the stairs and tend to her, carrying bowls of thick cream of chicken soup or medicine, each in turn administered under the watchful glare of Maggie.

She had kissed the Blarney Stone, but she already had the 'gift of the gab', a trait my father inherited, too. He was a natural storyteller. The pact she made with the ancient ruin, I think, was not a pledge for eloquence, but a safeguarding of her voice, perhaps, of her speech which burbles and simmers through the years and reaches the tip of my tongue, her youngest granddaughter.

While at university studying film and preparing a soundtrack to some documentary footage, I recorded my father's voice, along with my aunt's and uncle's. A fellow student listened to these voices as they spoke about politics, food, clothes and TV. 'They have amazing voices,' my friend said. Objectified and enhanced by this process of recording, I heard things I had not heard before: long, slow syntax, breaths in odd places, gulps and swallows, clearing of throats, murmurs and saliva between my father's false teeth as they spoke in their 'accented' English, lyrical, with the general, sporadic cadence of Anglo-Indian dialects. I took the earphones off and wondered how I sounded.

Through the long strands of DNA, which speak to each other in the morse-code language of chemistry and biology, the gift of 'eloquence' bequeathed to Maggie metamorphoses into the unfolding of a rhythm of dialectical and syntactical, linguistic and verbal expression which resides within my own body. This, too, is a turn towards the cosmic and our shared psychic maps.

I arch my body and fold my arms backwards.

At last, I can taste the teak tree and its heartwood kiss.

II

Exedra

Silverwood, Surrey

Beneath the exedra, Silverwood. The trees breathe and I inhale the forest from its living underside. *Respirare mi hai tolto la parola di bocca* (You took the words right out of my mouth). Into your tunnel, my words fall out of me. Accented English and Indian syllables. Tongue behind the teeth. Rolling the vowels like a cinnamon leaf between my mud-soaked fingers. You, Silverwood, make your own chatter, through the jingle-jangle underground. And the whoop-whoop call of half flightless birds. You, another continent. Avenue of ancient myths and dead Roman poets. So, I give you my Carthage, my Dido, my Aeneas, lime water, a looking-glass on your walls.

My father's hands take out a packet of custard creams from a woodchip cupboard painted white and the pools results on the telly. My mother strains the rice over the sink and shakes Oxo cubes from their blue Tupperware box. My aunt's wrists above her head, hanging out her washing, then her flannelette nightie on the line and fluorescent pegs dance in the wind. Inside, she prepares a plate of samosas for the guests when my uncle's fingers check the tax disc on his car for the very last time. My father plants a rose for him and then, we plant one more for my father when he goes, too. My aunt is a house, is a home, so no rose. Yet still someone mows the lawn where you all stood. Someone's black-haired daughter, arriving off the bus from Guildford. Waiting for Virgil to offer up some new kind of apparition.

Even I breathe differently in the woods. The air is alight with dirt-track dust, beetle wings and even dragonflies. This is a faery enclosure, a William Morris tapestry, a

Stan Brakhage film. Brakhage's avant-garde masterpiece, *Mothlight*, is made out of the wings of insects whose long-dead limbs are brought to life, resurrected by the movement of the celluloid, and are thus seen to be animated against the 'light' of the projector.

Out walking in Albury, I meet an Indian painter in his mid-60s, Hoshi, who lives in a cottage in Shere with his English wife. They invite us in one morning after we see them clearing leaves from the roadside gutter in winter. We are touched by their generosity. Hoshi tells me he used to walk into the privately owned parkland on the Albury estate. Years ago, he would walk up to the house by the moat, sneaking in with his little daughter, easily able to pass through gaps in the hedgerows surrounding the hundred-and-fifty-acre estate. As if by magic, they would enter the private parkland via a tunnel beneath the woods. He shyly admits to this act of trespass. For people of the diaspora, it is doubly transgressive.

In *The Book of Trespass*, Nick Hayes calls the private ownership of land, from as far back as the first act of Enclosure in 1235, an exercise of power and a social, as well as literal, partitioning: a fencing-off of rural equality. For Hayes, the act of trespass is one of solidarity and dissent. For me, it is also a physical awakening: to cross one boundary and enter another, to orient oneself differently, tells us something about the nature of orientation and its very shaping of our lived experience. My friend, Hoshi, tells me his daughter, now grown up and about the same age as me, used to love playing near an entrance to a subterranean room, a miniature Roman bath, at Albury. He and his daughter would enter via a tunnel which cut through the hill in a place at the highest point in the parkland called Silverwood.

What if I now passed through this tunnel? Would it also act as a time-travelling portal? Would I emerge as a small girl by the water, my father at my side?

Though we do not speak of it, a few weeks prior to our chat, we had nodded at each other briefly from the deserted roadside, the aura of foreignness in both of us rising up and into a spectral, shivering cloud on the road. We tenderly touched its edges with our smiles. '*You seem as different as I am and we are both here in this strange hamlet!*', I say through the other side of the cloud, not in words, but as stillness. Like the shadow of an oryx in an orchard.

Like Hoshi and his daughter, I also exist as a 'foreign' and unknown presence in Albury's Grade I Listed John Evelyn gardens which remain privately owned. As a resident, I have access to the gardens, a condition of my temporary home. It is thought that the diarist and gardener, Evelyn, built the tunnel, or crypt, which goes into the hillside in Silverwood from an alcove recess, or exedra, as a homage to the *grotto vecchia* of Sejanus at Polsilippo near Naples, visited while on his Grand Tour. Yet, it was also Hoshi's tunnel, it belonged to him and his daughter, her childhood secret which was as much a magical tunnel as a portal into an otherwise coded world of privileged ownership (of history and knowledge), 'hers', forever. To me, there is something very beautiful about that.

As he worked on his designs for the Italianate garden at Albury, Evelyn must have known the story about Virgil, the Roman poet, and his creation of the tunnel in Naples, which is also his last known resting place. In just one night, the story goes, Virgil formed the passage between Naples and Pozzuoli, performing a feat of sorcery. Now I was at the mouth of the tunnel. I claimed it as my own and it gave me something back, it transported me when I needed it to; it elicited the greatest magic to overcome what could only be described as the end of my world. I had never met Hoshi's daughter, but I imagined her by my side, about the same age as I was then, the two of us peeping into that tunnel and waiting for its magic to spill out words, images, histories and knowledge that we would have had no right to as women at the time it was created in the seventeenth century but plundered now nevertheless. Our fathers beside us in this ancient underworld. In my mind, we were not the minor characters in this parkland's story, we were the only voices and its secrets were ours alone, whispered here in this empty parkland.

In spring, I sit high up on the lawned terrace at Albury and mark essays for University College London while a local woman, whose hair is like a halo of white nettles, and her sons in checked shirts and flat caps, gather near a sheepfold, readying themselves for the shearing. I imagine the weight of the wool, the soft crevice of their necks, and my arms around the bellies of sheep. Fingers deeper into their curls. Their hot breath hangs in the air. (It will be nearly a decade before I hold a newly born lamb, hundreds of miles away in rural Devon). I sit between the house and the land, looking outwards.

Unlike the humans which are fenced off, or fenced out, sheep are everywhere on this estate. Indeed, sheep are numerous in this particular part of Surrey, near the strange little river filled with trout (the River Tillingbourne). I have never seen sheep up close like this before and it is mesmerising. Between the grass and the bend of the river they move across the land at a stately pace. A collective, yet loosened wave of obscurity, not white as I had once imagined, but a gauze-gash rhythm of momentary movement and stillness. Coming home with shopping, I try to climb a gate in a field, hushing them, as I slip into the sheepfold.

The nearest shop is a mile away and part of that walk involves the avoidance of animals. I try to imagine I have simply stepped into a Gainsborough landscape, a giant cinema effect, a technicolour print, which forestalls my grief and pricks my senses in another direction. At this moment in time, my father will have three months left of his life. I know this won't work forever, but I swallow the pill, eagerly. I do not want to go back to the house in Hayes. I just want to run. We have to run. But then we keep doing it, we keep moving. Even my mother goes on a coach trip to Devon just after my father's chemotherapy.

During the holidays, we take over from my mother and settle again in my old bedroom in Hayes with its pastel-blue peeling wallpaper and strange chalk sketches I had once made on the wooden door. We rent a film from Blockbuster and eat a take-away. Months earlier, I had been watching Sarah Polley's beautiful film, *My Life Without Me*, which tells the story of a young mother diagnosed with a terminal illness, but unwilling to tell her family, instead recording messages to them. We see her little family gather each night around their trailer-park home (the mother is played by Debbie Harry), squeezed around a tiny table eating pork ribs soaked in milk. Gone by the time her family view her video, Polley's character decides to make visible her own absence. In doing so, perversely, magically, she keeps something of herself alive via the video image. The closing sequence of the film is a montage of all the places she had been, without her, empty landscapes. This is an utterly heart-breaking gesture which serves to peel back the curtain, the artifice of our small existence. Going back to visit my father was like seeing the end of our film, together, simultaneously 'here' and 'not there', I had exited that life and I was watching the closing shots, the empty spaces (me off-screen, he entirely removed). In the bleakest of Octobers, we had started living some of our final days together, father and daughter. 'Here' and 'not here', a chemical process of reversal, under-developed film, fading and blurring out of existence. It has a thinning coldness about it, this intermediary point, and there is no respite. From his armchair, he watches images of the inauguration of Barack Obama, America's first President of African origin. A kind face staring back, waving before the stars and stripes. My father has, at least, lived long enough to witness this. Then, the Olympics in Beijing, Usain Bolt breaks the 100m record in just under ten seconds; my father sleeps through most of this upstairs and my husband and I visit Suffolk and Devon.

Years later, I acknowledge the fact that I was running away from my father's illness. It was the choice I made: fight or flight, isn't that what they say? It was a kind of self-preservation, a survival instinct which only grew over time, but originated here. I go back to that room where he sat and I ask myself most days, 'should I have gone?' The answer is still 'yes'. Should I have sought help, shouted a bit louder? I didn't know how to back then. We had only just got connected to the internet, but any advice would have been helpful. How was I to know what to do? Our house was not large enough to contain a very young married couple, my mother and my dying father and his Jack Russell called Pepper. It was difficult at the best of times, but nevertheless, half of us had to go.

Yet the 'leaving' part of all of this is restless and unsteady. We go, then we come back. We visited each Saturday and I simply cannot remember what we did. I have remembered so much, but these Saturdays are almost completely blank spaces in my mind. I recall only arriving with our newly adopted Yorkshire terrier, Hockney, and keeping him in a dog crate in order to save him from being devoured by the hugely territorial Pepper. At one point, Pepper charges through the back of the garden fence which once backed on to an allotment space, but was then being developed into some sort of housing. She has seen a fox. We call out and my father waits anxiously by the back door. A few minutes later, I open the front door and there she is with her tongue hanging out and paws on the gravel. She had found her way home. I closed the living room door and went upstairs to take Hockney out of his crate. We were all struggling with our connection to this house.

Then comes the 2008 Global Financial Crisis, a catastrophic moment which catapults our country, and the rest of the Western world, into recession. This event weaves a cat's cradle of chaos around the country, but it barely touches the fringes of our existence: newspaper headlines, Obama's victory speech, the closure of Woolworths on the high street. I do not know if anything registers properly with my father at this point in his illness; I finally run out of words and their rivers of meaning. I can't seem to put my foot down on anything static, real, solid, relatable or relational.

There is a bag filled with empty beer cans and a peal of rolling blue and gold aluminium rings out as I gather the remnants. A softly spoken Macmillan nurse from Galway tells me to call the AA (Alcoholics Anonymous). 'He's not an alcoholic, he's dying,' I tell them. An image of the old polished parquet flooring in our living room comes to mind as I wonder what to do. I had cleaned that parquet flooring many times as I dodged my father's feet. I wonder what to say, but all I can think of is the parquet flooring and its perfect symmetry steadying, locking and blocking the pinball-like thoughts of disaster in my mind. Everyone else, it seems, is shifting themselves in other directions – the direction of vague acknowledgement and obliviousness. You see, it is not a question of how many months or years, because the nurses cannot say. They will not say. Then, I ask the only question relevant: 'Where is the cancer?' I am on the top floor of a car park in Ealing and I am peering down at the floors below. 'Everywhere', the nurse says.

I am strong-stomached and stoic, my father's daughter, but when they say the word 'brain', I go quieter. He has already had a stroke. I am twenty-seven and I know, then, that my father will not see my thirtieth year. I turn back to the stairs of the car park, fragments of information detonating in my gloves, my fingertips, as I shove then deep into my cheap, long, black felt jacket bought from H&M in Guildford.

Muted and moored in this paling and unadorned life, fatherless already, I watched his starlit breath through his last winter. The open palm of his hollowed hand reached out to me in a hospital bed draped in green sheets. He asked for me with all the vulnerability of a stranger adrift in their own homeland. He was not an overly affectionate man, but I knew he loved me and his final goodbye was a tender reminder that I had always been his baby daughter who had arrived late and shortly after the death of his previous wife. My birth dovetailed his sorrow and now this grief is passed on to me. I was his salve, but what will be mine?

His arm on the hospital sheets shows a thin trace of his tattoos – red roses and blue-black swallows ascending from his wrist up to his elbow – a souvenir from his long migration on the boat from India to England. Amongst veins and liver spots, skin loose about the bone, the inked swallows make their own migration and a murmuration separates itself from his arm. Stretching out a long black web of movement over my father's bed, the swallows are performing their dark aura, their shadow dance, spectral hoops on the ceiling, on the glass hospital monitors. A silent wheat field at his wrist: the swallows dart one last time. Then, the sound of my skipping rope, over and over, and child's shoes lightly kicking the linoleum. He gives me red, red roses he has cut in the garden.

He gives me red, red roses he has cut in the garden.

Finally, we are told that there is not much time left. Instinctively, I telephoned my closest and oldest school friend,

Selwyn, a few days before my father's death and we laughed like school girls as we boarded a bus which took us deep into the countryside and walked the kilometre of ancient oaks up to the old house where our flat was. Selwyn is from Sierra Leone and his favourite film is Nicholas Hytner's *The Madness of King George*. We flit from lines from that film to bits of Hindi as we enter the parkland, easily time-travelling between now and our teenage selves, as old school friends often do. '*Jaldee, jaldee*', he shouts back cheerfully, 'quick, hurry up'. Despite it not being his mother tongue, even he knows many Hindi phrases owing to the predominance of South East Asian pupils at our secondary school. 'Come on, it's freezing!'. A few years earlier, he had made my wedding dress and driven me and my father across Waterloo Bridge and up the Strand, to the chapel at King's College London where I was to be married.

We chatted as we promenaded down the tree-lined avenue. The black oaks and a rare Lebanon oak (*Quercus Libani*) looked like royal guards greeting us, a dizzying, virtuosic landscape we had only read about in books by Jane Austen or Emily Brontë. Up the stairs and into the stillness of our flat. The cuckoo clock chimed. My friend sat in our Ikea easy-chair and snoozed, disconnected from London life albeit with one earphone dangling from his left ear and his phone in his lap, scenes from Hytner's film flickering on its silent screen. Everything felt strangely fine. It was a vigil, but it was also a few days before Christmas and they were singing carols downstairs. We ran around and took photographs by the decorations, stopping under their glinting light, posing, voguing. We ate mussels out of a packet with some old wine from the fridge. With puffy eyes and dirty black hair, I tiptoed around the edges of a new life without my father, and what lay on the other side of that. The fringes, the thin threads of a new life were coming into being: our first house, a career, two children, all yet to come.

After a phone call in the early hours, we drove to the hospital in silence. Already gone, his small mouth tightened into a rasping 'o' with pursed lips and eyes to heaven, small and shrunken, a monstrous fate which I was, at long last, called to witness and claim as Death. Two of my loved ones, my husband and Selwyn, kissed his forehead and it was over. What to do now? The hospital kindly provides a list.

My mother – we took her home and bought some purple and gold Christmas decorations from Sainsburys. We made a spaghetti dinner. The saucepan caught fire. Fanning the singed air, we sat stupefied in front of the telly. At some point, the Jack Russell had to be taken out, but my mother had not the slightest inclination.

My husband had to go to work that night in Chichester, performing in Bryony Lavery's adaptation of Charles Dickens' *A Christmas Carol*. While I watched the cloaked ghosts stepping out into the audience and heard their chorus, with lanterns in their hands, I thought of my father's breath still in the air, in the living room, the smell of his brown leather jacket and tobacco in the clothes cupboard. His death would span my present, past and, as I write this book, twelve years on, my future, yet at that moment I was still a wide-eyed girl too grounded in the daily routines of life to hear his exiled ghosts at my shoulder. Of course, to a certain extent, I had exiled them myself. But my father had let them through the cracks. I was already looking at the world through an upward rising mist. Somewhere, my future self was walking under oak trees in Hampshire, hands around a newly born lamb in Devon, witnessing the parting of fields of wheat and a small child chasing a thunderstorm, a meadow with a fallen tree shaped like a dragon, or a Burmese lion.

My grandmother's hands spread a deck of playing cards on a table. Someone catches her hand. 'Patience', a voice says.

We sat in a sad little room with a green carpet in the council offices in Uxbridge and registered my father's death. I did not know, then, that repeating the same devastating thing over the telephone, endlessly over the course of two days, requires relentless confidence. I was trading in tears for pieces of paper; 'My mother received a humble education in Calcutta and cannot write very well at all, she labours over it. Neither can she cope with official matters while grief takes its hold so I have no choice in the matter.' Swallowing cold air, I picked up the receiver and curled the telephone cord around my wrist. How many ways are there to speak of someone's 'official' death to BT, Hillingdon Borough Council, the private pension company, the library? (that one's me because I did not return a book to Senate House at the University of London). How many ways to declare death? Too many.

We lived in the little flat in Surrey for a year, more or less, while my father was ill. When he passed away, we settled into our first rented house in Peaslake. Further southwest out of Middlesex via the M25, this move, a thirty-two-mile journey from my family home to a house I shared with my husband was incomparable with the kinds of migration my parents had endured, but a migration nevertheless. I walked and watched it all through the eyes of a curious observer. It was like a living picture, no, a living museum of Englishness.

Peaslake has a notable link with the suffragette movement which Jenny Overton writes about in her book *A Suffragette Nest*. While Emily Davidson was knocked down by the King's horse at the Epsom Derby, protesting for women's rights, just sixteen miles away in the Surrey Hills, this small village was proving an appealing gathering place for the suffragettes in the early 1900s. Edwin Waterhouse, a founder of the famous accountancy firm, observed from his house in nearby

Holmbury St Mary, that Peaslake was becoming a meeting place for suffragettes in 1912 and there were at least fourteen other inhabitants of the village with suffragist inclinations. Amongst the bracken, these women were making Surrey radical. Walking amongst the footsteps of the suffragettes, my view of this place sharpens. I search for the index of these radical thinkers, their ghosts amongst the yews and the sloes, the dip in the valley where the air stills. I look at this film set of pretty cottages and country houses and realise that it is another world, a gilded enclosure.

Six months after my father had died, we moved into a terraced house with pretty wooden windows and a heavy oak door. It was the summer and this was our first proper home together after three years of marriage. The flat we had previously occupied barely consisted of proper living quarters with only a two-ringed hob, a makeshift fridge originally intended for beer and no washing machine. I put a shaky old table by the window, and dressed it with a tablecloth. I lit two candles. We ate looking out at the uninterrupted spectacle of the trees at close quarters, all vertical, white and ashen whittled lines ascending to the sky. It was a holiday in Surrey. The living room had stone floors and at night it was bitterly cold, but we fell in love with this place. For my twenty-eighth birthday, our new neighbour Jackie buys me a lavender bush (*augustiflora*) in a simple glazed pot which goes on to live with us, from house to house, for the next ten years. That was what was fostered here, a sense of family before we even had one of our own. Years later, Jackie becomes our first child's godmother.

The house faced a dense forest called The Hurtwood and the trees furnished this valley all year round, the spaces in between filled with murmuring sunlight which was at its most beautiful in the evening. Cyclists cut through the trees and we dodged them as we set off into the village. It was silent except for the call of cuckoos, a sound I became accustomed to as it settled into our daily lives, like the slow spread of a blackberry stain. It was weird and unnerving. I was used to the sound of airplanes taking off near Heathrow airport and unending traffic, what my father would call 'street wallahs' – Indian street vendors lining Southall Broadway – coriander and cassava leaves in the Indian greengrocers, the chiller section replete with packets of frozen samosas tucked between out-of-date Walls' Viennetta and Birds Eye macaroni and cheese.

One day just before dawn, my husband asks if I want to go to the seaside town of Selsey, a destination we had first heard about on Radio 4's *The Shipping Forecast*. Unfazed, I agree to this road trip, 'Ok, let's go'. Prompted, perhaps, by the early summer light and restlessness from all the changes we had experienced and, then, the expanded emptiness of the school holidays, we drive to this most southerly point in West Sussex and park the car near the beach. It does not feel real. Is this a *real* place? It seems fixed within the world of the radio, a couple of words which exist before and after other words which make up a list of points on invisible maps in the sky. We sit in the car for around thirty minutes and then we drive back, me half asleep in the passenger seat. Sometimes, it is best not to travel to places you already know in your heart, and live on happily with those lies or, rather, those imagined worlds. '*Sel-sey Bill*', my voice says, in the car. We were both searching for something, some sense of connection to where we were, or belonging, but this was not it, of course.

When we lived in Hayes, we used to escape my parents by travelling to Kent and Suffolk. We would stay in a static caravan and drive out to Dover in the night, tuning in to the French radio stations as shipping containers arrived in the docks and ferries drifted in the black water. Further across were Hythe and Dungeness with its lighthouse and little train that skimmed the periphery of this stark oasis.

You walk in a circular motion around Dungeness, the desert-like shingle beach which houses a Nuclear Power Station, a hamlet and an ecological site. A few months before my father's death, we had travelled to Kent and walked up to the strange dwelling which was once the home of the filmmaker Derek Jarman. At the shoreline, I heard my father's glass cabinets, which held his precious collection of Royal Doulton figurines, opening and closing, softly clasping shut like oyster shells on the beach, the ruffles of those porcelain figures strewn across the sand and the grit between sea glass and periwinkles; my father's reproduction of Gainsborough's *The Blue Boy* bleached by the sun and now monochrome, an x-ray on the shingle. My father's love of art was uninformed and simplistic, but yet so powerful in the way it seemed to move him, absorb him, even, affecting him in ways that the living could not. This was also true of his gardens in the various houses we inhabited, most of all our 1930s semi in Hayes. I still dream of this semi and I have always searched for a house like this with a garden like ours. I once googled our address and was immediately led to a lettings agency site in which there were photographs of our garden. Unbearably, our two apple trees had been cut back to their bare stumps, a few feet tall. My beloved trees, once climbed as a child, were crudely hacked to pieces.

Over the course of the next few months in our new home in Peaslake, I started to go on long walks and, again, I fought the pebble in my chest. How does a loved one's death make one homeless in a way that is entirely unattached to bricks, a feeling of homelessness because that person held within them the staircase, the door, the windows of your home. In the golden summer light, with the sound of crickets, cuckoos, oak and maple leaves under my feet, I walked up into the forest and the air altered. Speckles of light and dust particles floated and mingled with the heat and the smell of pine-tree bark, sap and rotting leaves, sweet and musky. Orientation became a movement towards the forest and its oneiric language. Limbs are heavy and clumsy, blunted, in the mute intelligence of those ancient branches.

Almost dark, inside the rows of silver birch trees, in the velvet shade, treading and tripping as any inexperienced woodland walker would, I took the first steps towards the village and I felt my breathing slow. It was hard to listen to all the sounds, so extremely loud, so dense. Imagine if you had never lived near a forest before, or lived, daily, with trees like these? Not ones you visited for a day, or picnicked near occasionally. I mean, to really live with the plain reality of these things. Tree after tree, differing in their texture and shape, bark peeling and curling like silvery sheets of paper, the earth full of insects. Slow. I could see the lights from our neighbour's house between the gaps in the birches. I felt the slight wincing fear of getting lost, fear of falling, but yet I carried on.

I had never been baptised. The vicar at the little church on Botwell Lane in Hayes thought it blasphemous to be born out of wedlock, but then there I was and they were not married yet. My father was very cross and never entered that church again. I cannot say I have ever felt the loss of this ritual, and my sense of self is not diminished, but there in the woods between Peaslake and Holmbury St Mary was the small gift: hope. In the thinning trees and the warmth of summer, it felt close to a baptism, not of birth, but of something changed and emerging from nothingness. In these chasms of light and noise, I was in a cathedral of trees, silently praying for a future and for the pebble in my chest to drop, drop deep out of existence and out of feeling. It was the happiest I had felt for a long time. It was ringing inside of me. It was golden. A quiet calm rose in the woods: a revelation. I needed this quelling feeling of stillness and the wind in the trees. Later, I wrote about forests and nature in an essay on a French film which happily gained me an award, received at the Sorbonne Nouvelle, Paris. Intermingling with nature, and making sense of that through writing, were intimately connected, though I did not know it at the time. It has sat deep within me, after all these years.

Was it the indifference of nature which made me smile, then, in the woods, or was it the knowledge that I was finally there, living on the periphery of that picture of *The Hay Wain* with which my aunt had cohabitated for over fifty years like a foreign friend in exile, similarly stranded? If that figure in the painting could speak, I am sure he would tell a tale or two about the conversations he had witnessed at my aunt's kitchen table. It was never taken down from her walls. Maybe it had occurred to my aunt that they were both in exile, and perhaps that is why she loved it, why it remained fixed to the walls of her kitchen. My aunt had never visited Constable's Suffolk and I had never visited a forest until I had first set foot in Surrey. How could that be?

After we had learned how to grow tomatoes, failing and then adapting, and collected blackberries in a margarine tub, the cold, no, freezing air arrived. It was so cold that I huddled beneath a blanket in broad daylight with plumes of very visible warm air escaping my mouth. The kind of scene you might see in a horror film. The dog tremored and curled under my arms, burying his head deep into my body, a body-cushion. I had felt the cold before, on walks to school as a child and when our boiler broke and we had to turn on the oven, but I could hardly move. I felt very stupid, knowing we were paying a fair price for such rented, decadent gloom. Alas, the stone floor was unbearable and the fire would not light, flames dying out while the room filled with acrid smoke from the newspapers we had used to ignite it. There was no food in the fridge and the growing silence of the exterior world beyond our terraced row was freakish, to me. It was dark and I could not walk very far.

There are, invariably, no street lamps in these semi-rural parts of England, perhaps because they are symbols of a modern existence which is unwanted and offends the eye – in my experience, if they do exist, their emission must be regulated to a soft, whitish light rather than synthetic LED illumination. A 'Lamp Black' pigment was spreading fast through Pitch Hill, the highest point I could glimpse from my small kitchen window. Inside, it was dim and unwelcoming. The summer had ended.

I telephoned Selwyn, who had just moved into a small flat in London with little money. We laughed about living off rice and tinned foods, but also feeling saved, happy to have our own homes, at last, even if we did not own them. I told Selwyn we had a full set of tables and chairs between us, across the two homes, if only we were to put them together in one place. Later, I brought a set of brand-new plates and cutlery to his flat, a house-warming gift in the middle of winter. Dylan parked outside Selwyn's flat in Southwark and ran up the stairs. We had all made it into adulthood, in a way, and were finally in possession of our own set of house keys. In the summer, Selwyn visits us and we drive over the Hog's Back between Camberley and Guildford to visit my mother in her new retirement flat. She has known Selwyn since he was sixteen when he used to bring her roses for Mother's Day. They had last seen each other on the day my father had died. She is very pleased to see him again, quietly navigating those memories while they embrace in her tidy little home in Surrey. Last of all, my father's Jack Russell is rehomed in Hampshire with another elderly couple in need of a new family member. At the dogs' home in Berkshire, my mother patted her gently and, in that last gesture, she closed the book on all of the things we had once called 'home'.

In December, we collected holly and lit a fire. Of course, to bring holly into the house is a pagan ritual and indeed this collecting of greenery, of boughs and moss, precedes Christianity and the fir trees associated with Saint Nicholas. I had never touched holly before and I arranged it carefully in a glass vase as we ate roasted potatoes and chicken, the night before we were due to leave for Berkshire (my husband had started a new job at a school). Against all odds, some more impossible than others (my father's lung cancer, my class, my heritage), I finish writing and submit my PhD. (I know all too well about the many students who give up and, still, there is a whole year to go before this process ends and I wind up in the halls of the Barbican in a black gown and mortar board). We ate an early Christmas dinner, a week before we leave, and I unveil pudding bowls filled with fruited suet. The brandy goes on and then they are alight. A year since my father's death.

On Christmas Eve, we packed the removal van and slid the Christmas tree in sideways, a bulbous spruce which shimmied inside the rocking vehicle as we departed. The first thing I saw as we drove towards Berkshire was a steep vista of conifer trees and sloping hills. It was dark and a set of red lights circled a high Victorian building, the high-security hospital also known as Broadmoor, just visible as we crossed a roundabout and entered the modern estate which would come to represent our home for the next year or so. After months in the woods, deep within the trees, we would be living in a populated town with schools, dental surgeries, phone shops and car-repair garages. Most of all, there was a Blockbuster rental store on the high street. After almost a year and insufficient internet speed, I could rent a film on DVD.

We arrived in Sandhurst, near the school where my husband taught music, with streets covered in thick snow which glowed in the dark. I had to readjust my vision, looking at unfamiliar objects and their contours which, somewhere deep inside of me, represented modern life and not the hermit existence I had clung on to as I finished studying and mourned my father in Surrey. I had spent so long in rural Surrey that I had, rather comically, forgotten the shape of late-twentieth-century architecture and its irregular embankments of square-shaped detached homes, chalet bungalows and narrow terraced homes with composite plastic-and-steel-front doors on large housing estates with their neat roads and pavements, conifers and garages with sliding doors. These, back then, were a bluish hue under the artificial light of street lamps; as they came into view from the passenger seat of the Luton van stuffed with all our possessions, my heart leapt. It was civilisation and, to me, it was glorious.

The months passed and I began to look upwards, into the trees again. I was drawn to Broadmoor, and I listened to this 150-year-old-relic, buried within a forest in which tall trees entomb it; the bones of the building seem to be vibrating like stifled breaths. There is a weekly wailing emitted from speaker systems strategically placed around the surrounding areas; this is the warning bell, the rehearsal of an alarm system whose air-raid-style screams confirm the asylum is secure. Occasionally, the whirring noise reaches a crescendo and metamorphoses into an intermittent scream so loud it can be heard for miles across several towns. At night, this red-bricked 'keep' is lit up like a constellation of itself, dots of hundreds of lights blinking, perceptible from the roadside. The hum continues through the night, while electricity pumps orange low-level lighting over manicured grounds, playing fields and a little farm.

I watched the strange totem-trees, the Wellingtonias in Crowthorne and the pines up at Wildmoor. I walked across a dry lowland heath and valley bog whose habitat contains unusual varieties of plants and birds, circling above a large housing estate on the edge of Bracknell. I saw a deer walk out into the road in broad daylight. One evening, we drive through the woodland between Surrey and Berkshire and we listen to 'The Lark Ascending' by Ralph Vaughan Williams, one of my husband's favourite English pastoral pieces. I hear flight within the trees, small circles of flight. My face against the window of the car, the spear-like trees reflected in the glass. The birds, the swallow tattoos on my father's arms, inked in blue, blue ink, inked the sky and then spread slowly, staining the night, my eyes shut tight, a blue-black mourning and an ascension. My father had never heard this piece of music but here, in the forested roads between Frimley and Camberley, I felt it was his.

Kanchenjunga

When my father died days before Christmas in 2008, I plunged my hands into the pockets and lined crevices of his old leather briefcase, grasping objects and letters stamped with official watermarks, dates and numbers. Then, there I was, a glossy picture folded into a small pocket, around five years old with a bowl-cut head of black hair, standing proudly on the patio in front of a bright-orange-and-yellow play tent. Beneath my feet were our chickens, maple-coloured flares of movement; ours, because my father had once dreamt of owning a farm. Folded neatly next to this photograph were postcards and transcripts, an accumulation of documents over half a century old. One of the objects was a postcard which was obviously a colour-tinted photograph of what seemed to be the Himalayas. A line of burnished turquoise with a skirt of snow-capped mountains, like folds of a wedding dress. Dark foliage blossoming below the translucent white rugged terrain. The tinted colour is fading and the card on which the image is printed is crimped at the edges. On the back of this postcard is its proper description: 'Kanchenjunga' (an English spelling of a word whose phonetic pronunciation reflects its Tibetan origins), the world's third-highest peak. This, I know, is the view from my father's boarding-school window, more or less: his version of home.

My aunt had once told me that the legendary Sherpa, 'Tenzing', knew our family, and he had visited her in their kitchen in Darjeeling. Tenzing Norgay, of course, went on to climb Mount Everest with Sir Edmund Hillary. All these mountain ranges and foothills swirl around inside of me. It snowed a few months after my father's death and the forest in Peaslake was like a Swiss mountain range. Though no one can confirm this, I do not think it a coincidence that my aunt Adelaide's first daughter is named Hillary, born in India around the time Norgay made his ascent.

How to take this knowledge of a particular place, of India, to London, as they did? How to reconcile the conditions of the wind and the stillness of the ice in Kanchenjunga with the drizzling rain in England? What happens to the body when the language of the weather shifts so dramatically that it is as if a finger is constantly tapping your left shoulder? *You cannot measure my force,* it cries, *I speak in a different cadence from the North Sea and the Atlantic Ocean, a different continent of Indian storm clouds and roaring drifts of mist across the River Lee and the Thames. Tap tap,* just there, a tiny finger on your shoulder, because it haunts you, this difference which you cannot truly name. It is an unspeakable loss, this loss of feeling associated with the meteorology of a place.

It alters our breath, this weather of ours. From the prickling frost to the rapturous skies, quickening clouds and milky light on window ledges, slow breaths in Indian summers, we called them, as the rains fell in Hayes and we stood on the grass, barefoot. My father poured lemonade into beer and wore a vest while he mowed the lawn in the sun, but then there always was the sound of the cricket bat against the wicket in Darjeeling, the wood being oiled, slow, slow, across the grain, exhaling along with the sounds of the beetles moving beneath leaves, the sound of the wind as he lay under the shade of a Banyan tree. The idea of Indian weather merged with English weather and everything else in between.

The weather is part of the story of immigration, it is the thing connecting mind and body, memory and feeling, to one particular place and destination and, for Virginia Woolf, this is especially cinematic:

This incessant making up of shapes and casting them down, this buffeting of clouds together, and drawing vast trains of ships and wagons from North to South, this incessant ringing up and down of curtains of light and shade, this interminable experiment with gold shafts and blue shadows, with veiling the sun and unveiling it, with making rock ramparts and wafting them away ... One should not let this gigantic cinema play perpetually to an empty house.

Which 'curtains of light' were glimpsed from my father's window in Darjeeling? Which 'blue shadows' fell on his playing field when he tapped, tapped the bat against the wicket? The imagination grows over time and these images play out, I think, surely, in my father's dreams. I would often watch my father by the single-glazed windows of our home, tracing his finger over the condensation, deep in thought, agitated if I interrupted him. He would say, 'We need to get these windows replaced', but I knew he was thinking of other things. The way rain felt in India? The thin crown of ice he could see fracturing at the top of the mountains, changing daily, momentarily. White mist.

My father knew the Lebong Cart Road in Darjeeling, the monsoon season, cardamom pods flaking in the heat, the sweet grass smell of the tea plantations. In Darjeeling, the soil is sandstone which shifts and shudders during earthquakes, the grass is lush. Was it a bitter disappointment to arrive in England? Why didn't I ever ask him this? Was every happiness always tainted by this confusion of spirit, of mind, of place and love?

In hospital, he tells me he went swimming that morning and I have the sense to remain silent. Usually, I would protest and correct him, of course, always the contrary child, but I looked at the little bed he sat on and slowly smiled. Through a haze of morphine (much like Ondaatje's Hana and Almásy), we begin to exchange stories. I imagine, he recalls swimming in India. His body remembers. It is the old ways which we turn to, perhaps to buoy us, to anchor ourselves in something true. He was a boy in the water. How could I deny him that? Months later I would find a tiny black-and-white image, about 4cm x 4cm, of my father at around the age of eighteen, neck deep in rippling water moving outwards, towards the edge of the frame, a close-up of his body submerged. Hair slicked back, his gaze fixed on the camera, proud and charismatic, as only a boy of that age is. There were two girls and another boy either side of my father. 'They were only friends with me so that they could have use of my sister's pool in Shalimar', he once said, bitterly. Yet, now he goes back there. He sits in that square of light in the pool and its oscillating movement, a strange portal in the manicured lawns and rose gardens in the grounds of the home of his newly married sister in India. All of time is peeling and puncturing the present. I sense this somehow and I leave him slipping, free-falling through those layers. Meanwhile, I swim up to the surface of things. I cling to the present.

So it was that I found myself lying to him. I would tell him he was doing well, he was looking well. All the time, the lies widening the gap between us. It is true, the lies we first tell our parents are the initial signs of adulthood, like the brightening of pigment in the plumage of some adult birds during mating season. Lies told to parents usually enable the desertion from childhood, the escape towards desire, the songs of love and its intricate vocabulary of disappointment. Lying is a primal instinct; it sweetens the thrill of autonomy, newly found in the flush of youth. In the skin of a liar, the world opens itself and yearns to be touched. But now I lied only to protect my father. I lied and told him he would be well and he would swim again, I was sure of it. I pass him his glasses and refill his water. This is the only truth which exists between us now and, minute by minute, it divides itself into atomised parts. Movement becomes time, the last we have of it together. My refilling a glass of water is a simple, necessary act and a truth we can both accept here, so I go on refilling the glass. He goes on swimming in the pool, which was actually a movement through time.

Romulus

Up a tiny, cramped staircase, in a narrow hallway between the Film and Philosophy departments at the Strand campus, King's College, London, I see a glow of a desk lamp in an office and I hear an Australian accent. I am curious, so I go in. It looks warm in there. The door is ajar and I see a sofa. I realise I am extremely tired. Could I sleep there, I wonder. The sign on the door announces that it is the office of the Professor of Moral Philosophy, Raimond Gaita. We have not met, but I know he visits in spring and goes back to Melbourne in the summer. He is kind and lets me talk to him about a philosophy-based event I am organising. He tells me about his father, his grown-up children, and his book *Romulus, My Father*. He hands me a copy and I take it. *Romulus* is about the way lived experience alters our relationality with things, it is his song to his father's way of being. We meet a few more times, or rather I gate-crash his office space, and we talk not about philosophy, but about parents, friends. He tells me he doesn't like big words like 'ontology'. Laughing, I ask: 'What do you call it, then, what you do? What is the use of philosophy?'

Raimond tells me he is recovering from a stroke and he asks me about my father and his illness. They are a similar age. Again, in the New Year, Raimond enquires after my father. The words come surprisingly easily to me: 'He died.' I see the shock on Raimond's face and realise it was not the kind of information he was expecting. Raimond goes to teach in Australia and I don't see him again, but our conversations have stayed with me. He sent me a copy of the film of *Romulus*, directed by the Australian actor, Richard Roxburgh. It is beautiful and I keep thinking about father, but initially I put a distance between that subject and my recent loss. Then time passes and I return to Raimond's book. Though I had not realised it at the time, the gift of this book was profound.

Born just fifteen years earlier than my father, Raimond's father, Romulus, was rather like mine in that he was an immigrant and had survived the trauma and deprivation of the Second World War. Romulus arrived in post-war rural Australia from Germany; he was of Romanian descent. He found a new home in 1950s Melbourne with his wife, Christine, travelling via a migrant ship, the *SS Hersey*. On the eve of Raimond's parents' departure, a woman read his father's tarot cards, predicting 'a journey across a large water, he would lose his wife and suffer greatly'. This was an awful prophecy which not only foretold Raimond's mother's suicide, after leaving Romulus and their son for another man, but also Romulus's own struggle with severe mental illness. Raimond's body of work, if you will, his philosophical teachings in books such as *The Philosopher's Dog* and *After Romulus*, which develop in dialogue with Emmanuel Kant and Simone Weil, explore compassion and love, and how we are conditioned to involve morality in the ways that we love. Above all, Raimond's work is informed by his father's life and constitutes various ways of bearing witness to that.

My father had witnessed atrocities as a child and, like Romulus, I'm sure, suffered deep depression, though he was never diagnosed. I come to this realisation after he has gone and it is a simple truth: I saw the shifts in his early morning rituals, still, as he sat and glared with an Old Holborn roll-up, his lower lip pursed. Expressionless. Tired. Hazel eyes with amber rings at the centre. Hours passed when I was not permitted to talk or interrupt him as he read his newspapers. Abrupt accusations and criticisms which were harsh and bluntly aimed at me. I shielded myself with the love he gave me, in small, but faultless measures.

To temper the grief, or pain, he sought out the giddying elation of the bookies, the horse races, which grew from his childhood love of poker and his first wife's pigeon-racing family (bets placed illegally through the letterbox). With a fiver in his pocket, back home with a whistle and a skip, he told jokes with great style. He laughed until he hiccupped. His false teeth gleaming. How does humour co-exist so completely with grief? *Pathos.* Why is it that my first maths lessons were betting odds written on the back of the *Daily Mirror* sports section?

'If I give you five pounds to put a bet on and it is a five to one win, that's £25.'

'What if we split the odds? What if I bet each way?'

He would give me £5 of his winnings and I would calculate how to spend this in Woolworths. If he won, we would also buy a Chinese take-away in celebration. When my father was made redundant from his job as a warehouse manager in his 60s, he a took up a part-time job at a local hardware store. He would visit the bookies daily and my mother continued her job as a dinner lady at my old junior school in Hayes. My mother never had her own money except for her earnings from that job. I wanted to know the secret to winning. 'It's to do with the grass', he would say. 'Different types of grass.' I do not know if this is true or not. When he raced pigeons in Acton, from the rooftops of his home with his first wife, was it the conditions of the air, the wind, and not the grass, then, which held the secret to success?

He rarely spoke of his first wife. He only ever spoke of their German Shepherd, Duke, who lay by her bedside, as she died from a terminal illness in their small flat in Acton. For a time, he lived alone in a bungalow, pruning roses, cutting the lawn. Even after twenty-five years, my father felt estranged from his new life in England, rather like Romulus had in Australia. He stared out into the lawns in our garden, he smoked as he watched a bird land on a rose bush. In detail, he would describe to me the monsoon season and the ice crystals on the mountains. He missed the climate of home, a particular sense of loss which Raimond describes so beautifully in *Romulus, My Father*. On his father's experience of the Australian landscape, Raimond writes:

> Though the landscape is one of rare beauty, to a European or English eye it seems desolate, and even after more than forty years my father could not become reconciled to it. He longed for the generous and soft European foliage, but the eucalypts of Baringhup, scraggy except for the noble red gums on the river banks, seemed symbols of deprivation and barrenness. In this he was typical of many immigrants whose eyes looked directly to the foliage and always turned away offended. Even the wonderful summer smell of eucalyptus attracted them only because it promised useful oil.

How had moral relativism shaped my father's world view? Yes, he had his own ethics and a natural empathy for the misjudged, the rebellious or the misunderstood. He was also uncompromising, he did not follow 'the crowd' and his truths were often harsh, non-parental, skewering me so much that I had no choice but to learn to fight back and counter his criticism, then sulk because, invariably, I knew he had a point. I know now that he had the inevitable apathy of a perpetual depressive: 'What is the point of going to school?', he asked childishly, as I applied for A-levels. I ignored him. In the Sixth Form, I was awarded a book token for my writing and, by chance and because she had just won the Booker Prize, I bought Arundhati Roy's book *The God of Small Things*, a story which instantly compelled me to think more carefully about my own identity and the shadow of India which haunted our everyday lives at home.

I was glad to be studying, though my father was still keen to get me into a supermarket, managing people as he did. I cannot blame him for this; after all, it was what he knew. So, there it was, I chose to educate myself and he could not care less. It was my triumph when I did well and got into university. He never asked what I did there, but he came to my graduation in London and listened to speeches, standing in a suit by the water features at the Barbican, and smiled, proudly, all day long.

My father remained rather childish and I think this was because he never lost that part of himself which was still a child in Burma. That boy was still there, split by trauma, still waiting to grow up peacefully. A ghost on the fault lines. Slippages in time and fixed in those spaces, frightened and tumbling through chaos. A kind of nihilism grew in him. Perhaps, this is why he sinfully ate the mangoes at the monastery and why he was expelled; this is why he never entirely respected authority. Yet he despised liars. He was only a child when he was held under brutal house arrest by the Japanese in Burma. As a teenager at boarding school, he would play poker, so much so that that word, 'Poker,' became his calling card, his schoolboy name. After his death, I found a photograph in his briefcase with a loving inscription to 'Poker', written by a bereft school friend, Brang Sang before he left for England. Many years later, my father watched the Channel 4 news and saw Brang Sang leading the armed opposition in Rangoon, Chairman of the Kachin Independence Organisation.

In England, my father married an English woman from Acton and lived happily with her, childless, but content for the length of a decade or so until her death from cancer. My mother had known my father from years before; he had been school friends with her brothers and, following their migration, both families continued to live within close proximity of each other in Ealing. My mother's first marriage was ending after many years and she would start to tend to my father, cooking for him while he lived alone, widowed. In this sense, it was a kind of homecoming and they would speak in Burmese to each other. I was born soon after.

Socially, my father would speak to anyone, entertain crowds, tell a joke. Impeccably dressed. Privately, he was detached, critical, highly conservative. He taught me how to have faith in my own world view. 'I don't care what everybody else is doing,' he would say. 'You don't have to think like everyone else.' He had no real care or admiration for any of my own school achievements, or failures, for that matter. I was measured only by my ability to play cricket or cut the lawn in our garden. Above all, he valued truthfulness and manners. At eight or nine years of age, if I smiled at guests and did not speak, he would say, 'Don't be facetious.' No, he was not the loving, benevolent father like the returning lord who greets his son at the end of *The Secret Garden*, or the blinded Captain Crewe reaching out to his beloved daughter after a long time apart in Hodgson Burnett's other novel, *A Little Princess*. But I knew he loved me and was capable of those loving gestures, or more, that I had read about in Hodgson Burnett's stories.

During one of our last conversations, he was tabbing on a roll-up with the window wound down. My father is driving back from the supermarket in his old blue Ford Escort and he says, one more time, 'You don't have to live your life like everyone else.' I ignore him. Heard that before. Then, without comment, he starts to undo his seatbelt and tells me that the car is failing, so he loosens his belt just in case. 'You know, I might have to get ready to jump.' He is a nimble 71, but I cannot imagine him rolling out of the car like Harrison Ford in the *Indiana Jones* movies, and I wonder if he is becoming too unwell to drive.

When I hear the click of the seatbelt, I ask, 'Where will you jump to?' 'The road,' he says, flatly. What is the moral work here? A daughter cannot easily appropriate her father's agency or autonomy, a child cannot easily subsume the role of the parent. The order of things becomes muddled here. This is an awkward navigation from the parented to the parent, from the cared-for to the carer.

I have been raised to listen, but also to question. Perhaps, all of what has come and the time between then and now, has been about the choices I have had to make. I have taken off my seatbelt. Are you expecting me to roll through this one, dad? I can't. I am frightened. I have no education (though, I am working on that), class, capital or status which holds any real power. What was the greatest possession he ever gave me? Was it a gold brooch in the shape of a bird from the jeweller's in Southall, or my first CD player when I was thirteen? No, it was my voice, but I was still kicking the stones beneath my feet, playing with the rubble, wondering what to do with all of that.

Mogok မိုးကုတ်မြို့

You do not need to be an archaeologist to feel the sedimentary layers of time slip through your fingers and marvel at an artefact you have uncovered. Neither need you visit a museum. What if you were simply out buying groceries? The object you find transforms you in infinitely small ways, over time, under your skin. Your heart is an ammonite. This object in your hands is not a dead thing, nor a buried thing, in many ways it belongs to you already. Your fingers are almost touching along the surface of it: a single strand of warp and weft. This is how one claims back that which has been absorbed into more Western configurations and contexts. You take them, you take them, and you grab greedily at their strange constellations of your other selves.

In my early twenties, I saw a Burmese Shan basket woven in navy, red and pink cotton, sold in a little shop near Hampstead station. This was the first Shan object I ever touched, other than my great-grandmother's bracelet. I found other objects in museums (427 listed objects at the British Museum), but these were never held within my own hands. To know of the physical texture of an object is to make sense of memories only you can access, tapping into these from time to time like clusters of hidden waterways which lie deep within your own heart-bound hydrology. Without these systems of contact, we drift and float, an eternal ghosting of the surface of all things. This characterises my conception of Burma.

Amongst other European and Indian nationalities, I largely descend from Burmese 'Shans', an ethnic minority from the Shan State in Burma. The Shan State is roughly the size of Texas and is a highland region, famous for its mountainous topography. Tea was introduced here via the 'Tea Horse Road', from the Yunnan and Sichuan provinces in China to Tibet, passing through Burma and Bengal. Here, bricks of Chinese tea were exchanged for Tibetan horses and this is possibly how tea was introduced to the Shan States. My ancestors would have most likely benefited from the tea trade and would have perfected the art of pickling leaves in order to make *lahpet*, fermented tea.

'Hill people', my father says, pointing to the trees outside our double-glazed windows in Hayes, his hand raised with fingers curved around an imaginary peak. My maternal great-grandmother was a Shan tribeswoman called Lucy Ma Aung and my paternal grandmother, Maggie's mother, was Parquala, who owned a house in Mogok, and was half Shan, half French. These women were the warp and the weft, the scissors and the needle, they inhabited the precarious, the seemingly unending dawn of colonialism, the silent spaces between continents. Despite all of these connections, my mother's family were made exiles with immediate effect on January 4, 1948, when Burma was declared independent from British rule, refusing them dual citizenship. Their European lineage (Scottish and French), though clearly combined with an indigenous heritage (Shan as well as Karen, another Burmese tribe), made them exiles in their own country. No doubt, Lucy was bidden farewell as they fled to India. My father's family were permitted to stay, but my aunt had already married and moved to Shalimar and my father was about to leave, too, for boarding school in the Himalayas – a new shelter which remained uncertain and volatile. Emigration was the next step because my uncle had found a job in England and, after all, the promise of England's opportunities seemed sweet.

Parquala King was my paternal great-grandmother. I know a little more of her than I do of Lucy. Parquala was Shan and from one of the Burmese hill tribes. She hailed from the Mogok region of the Shan states and it was believed she descended from noble ancestry. Mogok is well documented as the ruby region of Burma and 90 per cent of the world's rubies come from this beautiful mountainous place; the Burmese call these jewels 'pigeon's blood' rubies, deep-red in colour and almost opaque. Parquala knew there were very large rubies under her house. When her husband died, a German businessman, she refused to leave and stayed there until she was forced to move during the war, protecting her land with a rifle. My father tells me, proudly, she was an excellent huntress and rider of horses. Wild, I imagine her, a *femme fatale*, riding out across the Shan frontiers at dawn into some kind of Western movie with clouds of dust at her boots. Parquala's story ends here. I have no more knowledge of her except that she protected her rubies – their 'blood', it seems, deeply bound to her own invisible hematology.

Parquala's bracelet was destined to be passed on to me. Holding it in my hands, this 'pigeon' in the shape of a set of rubies flies about my wrists like the silvery birds which returned to my father in his loft in England. Home. My pulse beneath these stones and Parquala's presence, still, somewhere in between all of this creation. But very rarely do I wear this bracelet. I say, 'It's not my style, it's not my thing', but really the thing I cannot wear is its curse of grief and its attestation to displacement, to the tainted geology, to the extractive industries of rubies, sapphires, pearls and jade, as well as oil, fought over, binding an entire country to years of political unrest.

Years later, one of the world's largest rubies was discovered close to Parquala's home, perhaps even exactly beneath it. It resides in the Smithsonian Museum, Washington. An even larger, highly sought-after ruby is rumoured to have been given to Queen Victoria, decorating her Imperial crown. While she had no crown, Parquala's mother-in-law, my paternal great-great-grandmother, was named Empress Victoria Coty: a Frenchman's daughter born in Burma, descendants of a Parisian family, and named after Victoria herself. She was only an Empress in name, but the naming itself is important because it declares an allegiance with the Empire. Yet, surely, each time her name was spoken, the links loosened between continents, nations, crowns. The shape of a name is mercurial in the mouth of its speaker.

My forename and surname signify my European, Celtic, Gaelic origins (Welsh and Irish) and so it is that, at least on paper, all of my more complicated heritage is erased in favour of one narrative: the legacy of my Colonial forefathers. That narrative shifts towards them, and I have to listen more closely in order to catch the traces of other ghosts. How does it feel to be connected to lost ghosts, unfamiliar and thin in memory, the stories of Lucy, Parquala and 'Empress' Victoria? Half of the time, I simply forget. I am ashamed to say that it is easier that way, though I am becoming more attentive to these ghosts the more I grow older, the more I look at myself, as well as the faces of my children.

Shan women have been historically oppressed and enslaved, an ethnic minority whose cultural heritage goes as far back as the fifteenth century when the Mogols invaded their region of Burma. More recently, Shan women have been trafficked out of Burma. In response to such oppression, the Shan Women's Action Network was founded in 1999, a group whose members 'commit themselves to work for gender equality and justice for Shan women in the struggle for social and political change in Burma through community-based actions, research and advocacy'.

The Shan women in my family married European Colonials and disappeared into the invisible pages of a history book I cannot open. Their faces, no, their Victorian silhouettes, flattened, folded, collapsing, like a pop-up book with its pages clasped together, they were imperceptible and silent observers of history. I feel their concertina of folded movement, one lost relative after another at my back, me facing forwards while they patiently wait for the book to open again, revealing their ornate multiplicity. Or perhaps I am a Russian doll, harbouring my smaller, ever smaller selves; perhaps, there, at the very centre, is a Mongolian Shan woman as small as a nut, adorned in intricately woven cloth.

It is well known that the word Shan is a corruption of Siam or Syam. Siamese Shans are Northern Thai people and their war with the Burmese in the eighteenth century drove a rift, ever since, between the Shans and the Burmese. My father's grandmother had long black hair and her garden housed an ice house in which ice cream was made. The Shan women from the local village would carry my father as a baby to the market, trusted by Maggie, his mother, because they were her Shan 'sisters'. They carried my father in a 'papoose' like the cloth baby carriers we bought for our own children from Mothercare. Tied around their hips, the Shan women keep him close.

'*Shwe badaung*, that's what they would call me.'

I try to pronounce the words. He corrects me.

'*Shwe*. Shhh-way. It's Burmese. It means golden.'

'Golden what?' (laughing)

'Golden body, *badaung*, because I was fair-haired and fair-skinned.'

I stare at him, touching my own black hair. His hair is deep brown with only a few flecks of grey, smoothed with Brylcreem. (Dylan insists he must dye it in the night while we are all asleep).

Of course, there was also the very 'golden' *Shwedagon* Pagoda, one of Burma's most famous tourist attractions. In 1988, the Burmese political leader and Nobel Peace Prize winner, Aung San Suu Kyi, stood at the west gate of the pagoda and addressed hundreds of thousands of people, petitioning the military regime and calling for democracy (just a year later, the former Oxford graduate was placed under house arrest for almost fifteen years). As I grew older, I probed my family about their views on Burmese politics, but the truth is that they did not know what to say, or refused to acknowledge their lived experiences. They would occasionally see news footage featuring Burma, but it may as well have been reports from outer space, for they were living in Britain now and that's what mattered most of all. My European-Burmese maternal grandfather, Lewis, served with the British Army and was part of the Guard of Honour in 1947 when Suu Kyi's father, Daw Aung San, a man still celebrated today as the Father of the Nation, was assassinated. Lewis died in the mid-nineties, well before I could have a chance to ask him anything about his knowledge of Aung San.

When soldiers who fought in Burma are honoured at one particular commemoration at the Cenotaph in Whitehall, London, my father watches closely and becomes very still in his armchair. His eyes are wide behind his thick-rimmed glasses. There are no tears, but his mouth is pouting as if paused mid-way through a sentence, waiting to find the right word. Then, he says something I was not expecting.

He tells my mother, not me, how the Japanese tortured the female prisoners. He says they would throw very hot water at them while they were barely dressed, so clothing did not protect them. Water is sacred for the Burmese and the Water Festival, *Thingyan*, is an important part of their culture; it represents the washing away of the previous year's sins and disillusions, embodied by the act of throwing water at one's friends or family. The throwing of the water was now vengeful and full of hate as the Japanese soldiers scalded the women. It was a bitter assault on who they were. My father lived amongst such terror for most of his primary years, surviving, and learning about the darkest heart of the human condition.

After watching the ceremony at Whitehall on the BBC, my father gets off his armchair and picks up the phone in the hallway. He has gone to speak to his big sister. I can hear her soothing voice on the end of the line. She is always there and she barely leaves the house. She is navigating his grief, steadily, as she always has. Then, everyone goes back to normal and the BBC's *Antiques Roadshow* is on. I glance up at the Royal Doulton figurines in their glass cabinet in our living room and a family of elephants cast in copper hanging above our mantelpiece. I am trying to forget the images my father has just casually dropped into the air.

Later, my father visits the garden centre and he picks out some pink chrysanthemums to plant in our garden; he turns to my mother for guidance, for an anchor into the present. 'Those are pretty,' she says, reassuringly, evenly, 'pick those.' 'Yes, yes,' he says distractedly. His hands are still digging the earth in Burma, and I am orbiting him, expelled far out beyond the range of his grief. Neither of us can hear each other from this height. From the flowers in the garden centre grew tiny buds of hope. Fields of poppies represent living memorials to the dead, but my father's cheap flowers from the garden centre connected him, in more practical ways, to the soil and its promise of renewal.

Landmarks

I have often thought that books are a way forwards, a way to travel to places you cannot visit: they are my maps to these unspoken and unknown places. So, in mid-adolescence, I found Suu Kyi's papers written during her house arrest and her broader writings on Burmese culture and the Shan plateau, the home of tea grown in hills, like the hill stations in India. Suu Kyi has been the subject of notoriety in recent years, no longer an unequivocable heroine, but criticised as an out-of-touch dissident; her party seemed, as far as the world's media was concerned, to side with a military-led genocide which involved the ethnic cleansing of three quarter of a million Rohingyas, a largely Muslim ethnic minority from Burma's Rakhine State. The Rakhine state is well known for its ethnic minorities including the Arakanese, which was the ethnic origin of one of my great-aunts, but this news of Suu Kyi is heart-breaking, my childhood heroine now publicly referred to in the Western world as a 'pariah'.

While I carried the idea of Suu Kyi with me through my childhood, it was the image of my father held by the Shan women and taken through the market which haunted me. Each time he told me this story, he reminded me of the words of my grandmother, Maggie. She insisted that he make a mental note of his 'landmarks', places he would remember in case he got lost, like a breadcrumb trail, but one founded on a kind of deliberate memory-making. 'Don't get lost, remember the sights,' she would instruct him. Did she fear he would be taken, or left behind? Did the Shan women protect him and is that why they were carrying him? He was born during the Second World War, but the Japanese had not yet occupied Burma when he was being carried to and from the market by these Shan girls. There would have been a tiny window of time during which there was some peace and this is when he was cared for by the girls. He was passed around like a treasure, the youngest child of their Shan 'sister'.

Just a few years later and he is not treasured at all, he is an infinitesimal cog in the machine of war, a prisoner until the age of around seven or eight. My grandmother, Maggie, and my aunt, Adelaide, have to cook for the Japanese soldiers. Adelaide is around seventeen (I do not know where the men are. Perhaps you can imagine where they are?). Both women and my young father (about the age of a primary school child when the Japanese occupy Burma) are under house arrest because my grandfather runs an operation whose work is to extract oil and the Japanese want full control of it. While he plays in the grounds of the house and avoids the glare of the Japanese soldiers, my father sees captured British and Burmese men, thin and hollowed, carving ornaments, tiny objects, from pieces of ivory, or human bone. At least forty years later, I discover these in my mother's shell-covered jewellery box; I am allowed to look at them, holding them between my small fingers. 'Are they teeth?' I ask. When I am a little older, my father tells me how he carried messages between Japanese officers, like the boy in *Empire of the Sun*, and he always smiles and tells me he was their favourite. He protects himself with this lie, confusing his familiarity with the Japanese soldiers, their daily presence in his life, with his earlier encounters with the Shan women, a confused memory only he can understand.

In my teenage years, I struggle on through adolescence, as we all do, and I try to make sense of my features. Fingers splayed against my face, I feel the faint scars of chicken pox, one 'O' shaped blemish beneath my left cheekbone. Radio on in the background. Posters of *The X-Files* and Kylie Minogue. I brush my hair and hold up a section of it, wishing it was lighter, wishing it was straighter. I do not know anyone who is Burmese, let alone Shan. I have no objects or possessions, photographs or letters, which help me to understand who I am, at least not now. Like my father's daughter, I perform a storyteller's trick, I steal an identity, an idea, a mango, or an English apple. This, too, is a betrayal, because I am silencing the parts of myself already missing, absented. So, I drop the Shan parts of myself and I become something else, like my father in his Hawaiian shirt in Essex. I am my favourite film stars (Helena Bonham Carter, Ava Gardner), pop singers (I once auditioned for a music video for the band *All Saints*). All at once, I am the wolf in *Little Red Riding Hood* in a school play, Snow White for World Book Day, but I am also called, by schoolmates, 'Pocahontas', 'Mulan', 'Titania' and 'Princess Jasmine'. My grandmother gives me a box of magic tricks and I wish I was the disappearing coin, the rabbit in the hat. How do I perform the trick I desire most of all: the act of becoming whomever I want to be?

I become too good at this lie; I have fallen into a trap. At the age of nineteen, I am about to start an undergraduate degree and I am overcome with fear. I can't make sense of anything. I do not make it to the first day of class. I am cynical about it all in the way that only my father could recognise, that is, if he would. My mother tidies up my bedroom in Hayes and tells me, 'You don't have go if you don't want to,' but I do, *I do*. I am the first generation to go to university and everything is fraught with uncertainty and the fear of failing.

I didn't go to university. Instead, I spent a year temping in offices across central London (again, another disguise, you can be whomever you want to be when you are only temporary). I worked as a receptionist for Panavision and stared at the old-fashioned camera equipment in display cabinets in the lobby, wondering why I was there and not at film school. I answered the telephone for a few PR companies and wrote stories in my lunch breaks. I protested on the phone to anyone who would listen, I didn't have the credentials or the capital to achieve anything. I drew storyboards at home with cheap paints in monochrome and bought second-hand film scripts of Kureishi's *My Beautiful Launderette* and *The Buddha of Suburbia*, Ayub Khan Din's *East is East*, Mike Leigh's *Career Girls* and Anthony Minghella's *The English Patient*. I taught myself these things and I sent myself out into the world while my parents continued with their routines, their trips with my aunt to the supermarket. By contrast, I headed towards the noisy chaos of life.

One day, while I am still ambling along and not at university, I find myself catching the bus to Ealing to see my aunt. On the way, someone hands me a flyer for a local theatre production, and I decide to join the amateur group, The Questors, who are putting on the show just around the corner from my aunt's house. I devour the experience. Here, I learn new ways to speak. I drop the MLE (Multicultural London English) and I learn Received Pronunciation, like Eliza Doolittle in one of my mother's favourite films, *My Fair Lady*, except I am my own Pygmalion and it is the idea of transformation I have fallen in love with. Hands in Fuller's Earth, muddying up and ageing costumes, feet in between the chalk lines on the stage, I stitch a Scandinavian apron for the teenage daughter, Hedvig, in Henrik Ibsen's *The Wild Duck* and mark up stage directions on dog-eared scripts. I make friends with a much older, bohemian crowd. They literally speak another language. I change myself from the MLE version to the RP version, amongst these other chameleons, and the teenager from Hayes with straightened hair and chewing gum disappears. I learn new words like 'Brechtian', 'Proscenium Stage', 'Stanislavsky'. I learn quickly. Then, because our director's father had died, and I had shown some ability, I find myself directing a play at the age of nineteen. It is a tough gig, but somehow I not only manage it, but we have a full house every night for the short, but momentous run of the play. I stand in the wings and tell a petrified actor, over ten years older than myself, to take a deep breath. *I* should take a deep breath, too.

In the winter of 2000, I fall flat on my face, apathetic, and sit in silence for the most part of three months. I grew bitter and anxious because everyone around me seemed to have something I did not; they were at a cruel advantage. I saw my parents eat instant Chinese noodles on trays in front of the telly and in that moment I was overcome with guilt. 'What had I done for them?' I asked myself. Some of this is delayed teenage drama, I knew, but it is also a lesson about flying too close to the sun. Like the over-zealous and naïve Leo in L. P. Hartley's *The Go-Between*, I had taken a ride down the haystack and fallen to Earth like a fool. I needed a break. At home in Hayes, I shy away from friends and when they call the house my parents answer the phone, telling them I am not in. I sit quietly and watch the world like a hawk on a ledge. But, then, I was never on a ledge, I had reached some kind of summit and I was about to take flight. Pathetically, I watched anyone carrying what looked like university or college equipment with jealousy. I had done it to myself, this injustice. I told myself the next time, the next year, I would be ready. Two years I waited to go to university and then I didn't ever really leave after this point, staying on as a lecturer in academia even into my fourth decade.

I meet my husband Dylan at the back of the London Coliseum. We are both working as ushers and at the stage door (he has finished studying at the Royal College of Music and I am just starting my degree at film school). Seven years pass, Dylan living with us, marriage soon after, and, still, we are at home with my parents during a time of great global economic uncertainty. Renting is very expensive and my father tries to put us off several times. There is much writing, teaching, studying. I grow. I find out, finally, how to start to feel comfortable in my own skin. Yet, I still searched for connection. I still searched for strength. I wanted to feel my great-grandmother's gentle hand on my cheek, pushing my hair away from my face and wishing me luck. Perhaps my parents should have done that; they did in their own way, but I was desperate for more. Sometimes, we have to propel ourselves in order to feel the line of our ancestors and their blood rising in our own pulsating bodies. So, I stepped forward.

I take a part-time job at The National Gallery for a while where I stare at a large tiger in a tropical storm, Rousseau's *Surprised!* Jobs on a few films helping production designers with props and sets, but all the while writing, imagining. I am an exile, a misfit, growing up and listening out to the new noises from the city. I learn the names of the streets of London, temping in offices and following Dylan to his concerts all over the country where I spend many afternoons as a tourist in places like Canterbury, Stoke-on-Trent, Cardiff, Rochester and then each winter, Birmingham, for the New Year concerts in the Symphony Hall (followed by New Year's Day concerts at the Barbican in London). I was learning and absorbing new ideas like alchemical processes which were quietly re-configuring who I was. Yet, I was still the kid from Hayes hanging out with Selwyn in his Fiat Cinquecento on the way to Ealing with a copy of Ondaatje's *The English Patient* in my hands.

During my late twenties, I walk past the local Blockbuster video store in Hayes with a handbag sloped over my lower forearms. Half-heartedly, a local boy passes and shouts out, 'Oi, oi, Mrs Thatcher does Hayes.' Not only does this unnerve me because I am the most unlikely Margaret Thatcher in many respects, but because I am left feeling bewildered by this statement and usually nothing gets under my skin like this comment does. I had imagined I would always fit in here in Hayes, but now I was being marginalised as something other, even if it was just the way I was holding my bag. Could it be, somehow, that the kid had sensed my 'out of placeness', or was it the way I stood, or my seriousness, my determination, even if he got the politics wrong? I laughed, but I remained fascinated by the peculiarity, and specificity, of that jibe, all these years later, not because it was offensive, but because it was all prompted by the way I had held my bag and, consequently, my body. I still had much to learn about myself.

'I want to know,' I admit, quietly, to the nurse's voice at the other end of the telephone.

And so we are back in the car park in Ealing Broadway. The Southern Irish Macmillan nurse is telling me where the cancer is in my father's body. I'm looking down into the atrium of the shopping centre from the balconied upper floors. Something dislodges the memory of my father as a baby, carried by the Shan women. I see glimpses of them in the atrium, their crimson shawls passing behind a corner and then out of sight.

'Remember your landmarks,' he told me as a child. The car park drops away from view and I enter a clearing in a forest in Surrey, the only forest I know at this point in my life. The seemingly preposterous, yet peculiarly relevant, idea of the Shan women in my family reveals itself to me. My ribs ache and I suck my breath in. I put my arms on my hips and bend over to concentrate on my pounding heart. Perhaps this is a hike in the middle of summer in England. Either way, I feel exhausted. Instead of reinforced steel and a concrete staircase, bushes evolve from the metal and on their tips are tea leaves from the Shan hills. I am standing in a tea plantation. It is not the kind of tea you smell when you open up a fresh box of teabags from the supermarket. No, this is acidic musk, sweet, floral, like gardenias and soil, lemon balm and mint.

Then, it occurs to me that they were picking tea when they carried my father to the market. Of course, they were crossing the tea plantations near my great-grandmother's house in Mogok. She had sent them to bring back tea.

In the spear-shaped tips of the trees, they breach their silence. Their faces peer out at me through English oaks and Burmese teak. Once, my aunt had given me a bracelet with jewels drawn from their world. I was never a Russian doll harbouring them, it was *me* they harboured, for they were my Burmese sisters, too. They were still carrying me, pulling me deep into their mountainside of truth. There was a whole world inside there. They carve out, from the full moon in an English meadow, a silver spear for me and they say: these are your old ways, and your custom, these will take the shape of the spear, and you fire this back at them, aim to splinter their prejudice, their lack of faith in you, their long, slow shadows across our kingdom. Look how far this spear travels.

The silver spear has become a Tibetan horse. She is running towards tomorrow.

Somewhere long ago, next year, a hundred years ago, last week, yesterday, my grandmother Maggie is returned her baby boy, Lambert, and he is untied from her sister's hips, held out in the air. His cheeks ruddy from the cool air in the mountains. Together, they smell the tea leaves on her fingers. Everything is sweet.

Strange geologies

My father was cremated in West London and his ashes placed in a small box within an olive-green bag. I am handed these at the end of the funeral, which I organise, along with a eulogy which, perhaps you'd like to know, paraphrases the opening section of this book.

At the service, I am still, like stones once skimmed and now lost at the bottom of the River Tillingbourne. Smiling, but still. My aunt is there, so I'm brave for her. Her little brother had gone, after she had protected him so long, through so much. Her loss goes further back than mine and my mother's, somehow, a mother's loss, which I accept here.

There is a trombone solo from my husband: Handel's 'Where'er You Walk'. I know this is a poetic, mythological aria which features in the opera *Semele*, but I cannot help imagining the idea of walking and begin to wonder about the nature of the ground we walk on. The ground, it seems, that I will have to break, if I choose to bury my father's ashes. *When did we walk together? Where did we go?* I imagined he was there in that ancient woodland in Peaslake, in the light which was golden, and I had daisies in my hair; he was at the curve of the road in Berkshire with the ancient hedgerows and Wellingtonia trees, in the divine cosmos of their shadows. *Where else? Was there, still, more to come, more to leave behind as we travel?* Ghosts travel, easily, through the borderlands of 'then' and 'now'.

Can ghosts still breathe, the little boy asks?

I don't know.

Shall we walk?

My father always had a dog with him; perhaps there is one

at his heels now. In the briefcase, I find a photograph of a very small, scruffy terrier with its tiny eyes squinting at the camera. *Was this a friend?*

Before he left for Darjeeling, my father caught typhoid fever. He lay in seclusion in a sanatorium. He became so hot that they shaved his hair. He lay still. Eventually, a dog belonging to one of the nurses followed her in and then refused to leave; it sat down beside my father's bed and lay on the bare floor. His hand reaches down and he feels coarse waves of hair. The dog does not leave until he recovers. His hands move in soft rhythms against its fur. The sharp tang of disinfectant is what they breathe in together in the darkness. The dog is his companion here as he reaches this landmark in time.

It was our dogs which made him venture outside. In the rain, they walked slowly, together. One of our dogs, an Alsatian pup called 'Tina', shreds his daily newspaper and deliberately deposits the chewed remains in his slippers. I wash the soil from their paws and I take the towels blackened by mud to the washing machine. I smell the damp tufts of hair between the soft pads of their paws. My father's tobacco-stained hands across the line of the dog's back, all the time talking as if I am not there, just a conversation between them. You run your right hand along an obedient dog's back and before you reach their tail and the end of their vertebrae, they usually fold their hind legs inwards and sit for you.

Between Surrey and Berkshire, I started to think about soil or, more precisely, sediment. I started to dig into the frozen ground in winter and I saw layers of clay, loam, sand and roots spreading under the moss. But it was only when we moved into our home in Hampshire that I started to look differently at the land. In Berkshire we had rented a home with a dead dog allegedly buried in the garden, so I never was inclined to start digging in that garden, which was also a grave. After that house, we rented another home on the Owlsmoor housing estate with a large, square garden. In the summer, I let speedwell (*Veronica filiformis*) weeds grow through the patio slabs and it flowered across the garden like a carpet of pink jewels.

I had known few gardens growing up. I once fell from an apple tree (my father once fell from a cherry tree). Climbing up the fences of our first home was a collection of prized, multicoloured roses, lovingly tended to by my father every summer. They were not his, but his inheritance from the previous owner of the house. Once, I discovered the treasure of some beautifully illustrated, quaintly descriptive gardening books tucked at the back of the cupboard in my bedroom in Hayes, near the boiler which was wrapped in wadding and breathable plastic. At the back of our 1930s semi, I tumbled and shook mud from the raised beds into old ice-cream containers and poured water from the rusty tank with a dripping tap, making mud pies and perfumed blocks of rose water and soil, while my parents sat in the conservatory and sipped tea. I was hours out there, in our fenced, urban garden.

I watched tiny horsehair worms in our outdoor water tank and touched the skeletal remains of a frog concreted into a neighbour's brick wall. I remember summer evenings helping my mother collect the washing from our clothes line and my father raking autumnal leaves from the back of the garden. As a toddler, I picked out carrot seedlings, mistaking them for weeds, my small hands, covered in soil and clasping sprigs of carrot foliage. Then, there was the French lavender and the long, twisting green beans that I grew as a teenager. I used to pinch the edges of dragonsnap plants, watching their 'mouths' open obediently. I would watch my mother's hands scatter rice for birds (which I now know is not good for them).

I said goodbye to our garden in the new millennium when I was nineteen and my father retired. We owed money on the mortgage and could not afford to stay so we chose a very small former Hayes and Harlington railway workers' semi around the corner for just over £100,000, carried some of my things down the road, and called it home. Not long now before my future husband joins us here. This house had one living room downstairs, a narrow kitchen plus the bathroom, and three very small rooms upstairs, mine being the largest after a smooth negotiation (I was going to university, after all, and needed the space to write). My father could not bear to leave his sister in Ealing, so he never retired to a thatched cottage in the countryside like the one in the painting he hung in our living room.

When we left Coldharbour Lane in Hayes, the canaries needed to be sold off. Their new owner arrived, but then someone didn't close the latch on the wooden door properly and they all escaped. Not a single bird was retrieved. We all stood and watched fifty birds spill out of the aviary and into the ether. Two men stood with nets above their heads. My father's face was smiling, he didn't care. Yellow confetti, winged darts, a spread of powdery clouds burst into the air and past our two apple trees. I shook the old birds' nests out onto the grass, unpicking their wiry innards with my fingernails. But the dead still lay on the floor of the aviary. My mother swept the aviary floor and my father stood with his hands on his hips by the roses. I witnessed their migration before our own from the home I loved, and now how many more to come?

In the garden in Hampshire, the sixth garden I have occupied throughout my life, I planted tulips. This was our first garden in a home of our own, and with my husband I tended our tiny patch of land. It was back to front, the garden larger as you entered the property's boundary because, years ago, this would have been a field and the back garden, a route for coal. My first awareness of soil and topography comes from the information report received when purchasing the house.

The PDF from the surveyor opens and you are presented with obscure maps of zones and territories surrounding the property you are purchasing, then, information about the nature of the water, the type of land your property sits on. We saw a pretty red-brick cottage on a quiet lane with rosemary arching over the door; the map offers up a survey, or 'search', which should indicate the value of the property and its habitable status. It is factual information which gets saved in a drawer somewhere along with the land registry certificate and the deeds to the house. If you explore further, like a private detective, you can request 3D models of Great Britain's geological mapping. On my computer, I hover the cursor over the map and zoom in to locate all the waterways, canals and rivers. There is a canal nearby in Odiham. Portsmouth, the home of the Mary Rose ship, is not far.

What is the geological form of grief? Surely, it is cast in stone, as are all those in the cemetery, or along the wall of remembrance. Marble, granite, we gift our dead these solid shapes which belong to the earth. But grief, also, is sculpted from another language and exists in the cavities of time, below the cracks, etching and hollowing out little recesses, loops and bellows, because memory is cyclical and it does not go out but in, retreating forever inwards. Imagine the circles of a tree: a cross-section of time. Our memories simply reconfigure themselves, a new gesture here, a forgotten phrase of a loved one, there. *Was it my father's hand on the spade digging the earth in our garden, or was it mine, Hampshire soil, or London clay?* A cool, inflexible piece of silver, coiling, and a line of sand, physically rattles through my grief, sharp and granular; they bore down into the deepest memories of all other things, the process of recall quietened by this movement, slow, slow, never stopping, just below the base line of existence. A tiger stalking me, its breath on my back.

We want to take his ashes to Darjeeling, back to school, but we cannot afford this trip of a lifetime so, instead, I open up Google maps, again, and hover over aerial images of Mount Hermon and the division of land around it. I can see it. I also visit not one but two Mount Hermon Alumni websites and I receive a message from an old friend of my father's called Tony; he sends me images of himself and my father in a swimming pool, sunlight on their faces. I have a growing desire to plant a tree there, on the grounds of the school but I do not know if this is even possible. I imagine going there and all the doors to time will fly open, a time paradox – he makes it home, after all these years. On the ground level, perhaps I see the window to my father's dormitory and inside everything is sparkling, a silvery mist. I visit the ledge of his window. Every day is about that ledge, in some way or another.

For now, I take the ashes and they sit beneath our staircase in their bag. But he also lives in my garden, in all the gardens I have ever tended to. He is the robin on the garden rake and, in years to come, the rose my husband plants in Devon. One day, we say, one day we shall take the ashes to India. Until then, he lives with us and silently witnesses the next ten years of our lives. It is strange to be handed this box, this object, and to know something must be done with what is inside – an unnecessary ritual, in my view. I know there is comfort to be found in this process of scattering ashes, but I avoid it. Now, he is long gone. But, still, we bury the box beneath a cupboard full of toys, old plugs and a hoover. He would not protest. He was never afraid of death (as you know, already).

The car alarm goes off one night and I wake from a dream.

When winter had passed and the sky started to turn from grey to blue, I began to prepare for spring, digging out space for poppies in our garden, where my father's ghost lived. Lux aeterna, a requiem in the garden. I stand raking the earth. We have a beehive here. It opens.

I reach inside. The texture of honey is familiar but the shape is not. The bees have formed a honeycomb around something and it seems to turn the entire hive a shade of scarlet. The octagonal shapes of the honeycomb wrap over an oval-shaped object – a kind of second skin around it. As the light shines in, the honey glistens and drips over something bright-red beneath. As the bees disperse, I poke the object very gently and see that deep within the honeycomb is an oval stone which contains the patterns of a starry constellation with billowing clouds passing over its curved topography. The honeycomb has been constructed by the bees around the stone, embodying its oval curves. It rolls forward and before I can catch it, it is on the grass and the honeycomb is split. The bees continue to flit about the object and the honey drips from it, sticky and flowing in colours which range from amber to deep red. A ruby, the colour of pigeon's blood.

Deep hibernation

I walk home through the trees and there is a mist of white beaded curtains dangling a few feet ahead of me, branches covered in frost. I hear twigs break beneath my feet. I look down for a moment, straightening a bootlace, and a face floats between me and the whiteness of the air. I know this face. It is the Green Man and he has come to claim me.

His lips are a thicket of oak leaves twisted into a protruding knot and his eyes are shining conkers. Above his waxen goblet eyes, deep-set eyebrows of thistle, thorn and briar; his ears sodden, trodden pine cones, his hair the colour of wheat fields on fire. He has the look of Zeus with tawdry bracken about his thick neck. Tiny seedlings growing from within his cascading beard. He is granular, grainy, more like a fossil than a deity. We are eye to eye in this tracking fog.

'You do not belong here,' he warns, barely opening his leafy mouth. 'What right have you to dwell under these oaks? You taste of something Other.'

'Where should I go?' I ask.

'Closer, here, into the fold. We can taste your sorrow. We can make you dream of only starless skies filled with never-ending songs and cherry blossom at your mouth.'

(I try to listen, but am distracted by the seedlings winding their way through his beautifully oaken face. The seedlings have become ivy through my hair.)

'Become us, accept the ivy. Accept our binding,' he commands.'

'No,' I whisper. I pluck out a strand of my hair and it loops and expands into a tree made of the blackest teak.

My great-grandmother's ruby bracelet is thrown into a

pond and it transforms into a banyan tree.

He disappears and I am left standing at the border, between the oaks and Otherness, between the ivy and the trees of my father's childhood. Now I become the border.

The borderline, sometimes known as the abject, marks the place on a woman's body where children come into being. They wrestle forth, between all of the spaces, inside and out.

After the birth of our first child, Inigo, we continued to live in Hampshire for many years, the longest we have ever lived in one house as a family. Daily, I began to walk the mile or so down from our terraced house (fifteen-to-seventeen-minute walk) to the shops or the nursery and back again, with and without a buggy, and this goes on for the duration of around eight years. I rarely leave this village, bound to childcare, to routines, to tiredness, and more tiredness, to deliberately adorning myself with blinkers because this is the difficult bit, slow and frightening, but also full of unmissable moments of joy. Now and then, I take the train to work or to the Thames. We perform great breaststrokes of physical and mental agility through these waves of time, in and out, we breathe deeply as we steady ourselves, working, caring, cooking, washing, 1 a.m., 4 a.m. Broken sleep which becomes a habit even when there is nothing to wake us. 1 a.m., cricket on the radio. My father is still there, in Hayes, an imprint in time: downstairs on the armchair with an earphone in one ear and a roll up in his hand, elbow against the armrest. India are playing. *Dad, did they win? Not yet, not yet.* 4 a.m. Our neighbours' outdoor lights go off. The dead of night. A starlit spell which you work, or weave, or which works you, gentle, gentle, but to the bone. *Dylan, I can smell tobacco.*

I had never held a baby before and I was anxious. What did I have to give? Now, I know the question is, rather, what did I have to *lose?* Because, you give everything to your children and it never stops. You are left with nothing;

you relinquish your body, your blood, your milk, then your pride as you begin to care less about a lot of things. Next go your passions, because you do not have the time nor will-power, your breakfast, your lunch and your dinner, your foul moods and your joy, your dancing, your singing, your strength, your weakness, your elbows and your knees, your back and your wrists, your eyes, your mouth, your breath. And all of this, you give willingly, gladly, like a dumb fool. Your instinct, before you even think, is to protect and then to shelter, to nourish and protect. Then, if you are lucky, you pass on your histories, your words, your images, picking up leaves or tracing a finger over a painting or photograph, you teach them small things, expanded in your shared and tightly focused universe.

By this point, you have probably surrendered yourself. Then, when they speak to you, after all those months of not speaking, or silently gazing into your face from their buggy, when they walk on their own and they start school, they pass back, for a moment, what is rightfully yours: they do not need you in such totality anymore. But the person, the shape of being that they have passed back to you is no longer recognisable. You have changed. This is the way of all love, which is an often unintelligible reciprocity. An infinity loop, a milky way and a cosmos, a planetary system. A whole other movement, continuous and unrelenting, unexplainable (though, here, I have tried).

Birth is another thing. You cannot hold that against them.

It starts well. It is around 9 a.m. and Melvin Bragg is on Radio 4. Eight hours later, the situation is very different. I find myself in the awkward position of a home birth, deliberately elected (fearful of hospitals), but then with no medication and pushing for nearly two hours. My heart rate slows and everyone looks worried. The baby's heart rate slows and they call an ambulance.

Two hours of this and I was still there, trying, fighting. My husband shook his head. The baby was very badly stuck. Determined, I clung on to consciousness in an early September heatwave, nearly two weeks overdue and on the floor, just yards from the pub garden further along our terrace, filled with people drinking Pimms and local ale. Quietly, stupidly, I visualised our garden in Hayes, I breathed in as I imagined my father walking down the path, me walking past all of the flowers in the beds, one by one, an incantation, as I breathed out. An incantation. *Primula vulgaris. Dianthus. Lilium.* Weeds between my fingers and daisies round my neck; my muddied fingernails scraping along concrete, a friend from across our street in Hayes circling lengths of a dirty orange, rubber skipping rope around my waist as I pretended I was a horse. The knot around my stomach tightened. Closer to my ear, the air whipped over and over me as we skipped, light and taut, over and under the rope. A secret garden, perhaps.

In our cottage in Hampshire and undergoing the process of labour, I started to bleed everywhere and a blood vessel burst in my left eye. Two fairly relaxed midwives clambered on to our bed and checked my pulse. Ten days before, my husband had been in hospital with suspected viral meningitis. I was insulted by a consultant who asked me if I knew what the word 'empirical' meant. I visited my husband in the small hours of the night in an isolated room, wondering when I was going to go into labour and be in the hospital myself. Then, swapping over, I was finally in Frimley Park hospital, giving birth, but anaesthetised, by the light of the moon. At 9 p.m. on 2 September 2012, I held Inigo, or rather he was clamped to my side, skin to skin, and I tried to say hello, the sounds of the skipping rope still ringing in my ears, or some other kind of rhythm bounding and somersaulting, all at once, over the years, under the land, over the years, under the land. The back of my head bowed down as I held him, tucked into the neckline of my dress. I could not see very clearly, my left eye a bloodshot mess and raw about the bone.

Inevitably, Inigo sleeps in our bed, or at least spends a lot of time with me inside it, so I wake into the cold morning with his tiny foot kicking the side of my chest in coils of sharp movement under the sheets. His wriggling weight up against the borderland of my left shoulder and my ribcage. His breath on the side of my face bearing the faint scars of my own infancy. Daylight.

When Inigo is around six months old, at the start of spring, we plant a pear tree and an apple tree in our tiny garden. The boy who sells us the trees in the local garden centre is Nepalese. I tell him my father lived in Darjeeling and he is fascinated by this. He tells us he likes to dance and he wants to perform on stage. My husband takes out his trombone in the garden centre car park and plays a few notes. The boy's gentle, delicate hands usher the trees into the back of our car. He is softly singing as he moves about light-footed, smiling. He wants to be a classical dancer, but for now we are his only audience in this garden centre off an A-road near Farnham. The apple tree blossoms the following year and the pink cups of petals drift downwards, over our purple *buddleja* and the *ceanothus* shrub (*Italian Skies*). When he is old enough to stand, Inigo plays in our small garden and the world outside is partially abandoned. *Goodbye*, I say, *I have disappeared into a wood, a hooded woodlander with a baby in the twilight*. A faerie spell.

A tiny mouth opens in the night and we rock sleepily to the sound of the refrigerator, the BBC World Service, the cricket. It is a deep hibernation of work, child care and sunny survival, because we were lucky, after all, to live in what appeared to me like a little postcard of the dream my father had of England. We spoke to everyone. When we finally left in 2018, all the glorious voices and faces of those twenty-first-century villagers seemed to me like a strange re-enactment of Dylan Thomas's *Under Milk Wood*, with their songs of little triumphs, fears, laughter and school runs, pubs and forgotten, cold cups of tea at baby groups. Here, also, I found great warmth and spirited kinship in the form of many women who were old enough to recognise I needed help, or clever enough to respect who I was, who we were, and that we were different from the usual lot (a writer and musician). One of the much older mums, an engineer with a PhD, pairs up with another from our road, a lady who drives a milk float, and together they help us clean the house before we leave. You know you are loved when people willingly arrive to clean your home and wipe the dust from your skirting boards while your children dawdle near a removal van.

Eight years here and every day is a marvel because there are pheasants hanging in the butcher's window, thatched cottages and duck ponds, a cricket green and children on scooters, bikes, walking to school along lanes with pretty cottages and geese flying over our heads. This is, of course, a highly decorative veneer, with its own ageing patina, also: a bewitching. This is a London suburb in disguise. Yet, if you look closer, you can see the framework of the old ways, the innkeepers, the landowners, the ironmongers and the joiners, carpenters and firemen (there is a fire station) whose families have settled in the village for generations. Then, the trains bring along IT workers, city traders and sales people. Five hundred new homes are built and I watch the hedgerows get pulled from the earth by diggers and yellow JCBs with huge buckets levelling the ground. From the estates, children who come along to church meals with their parents, lonely widows, single mums, anxious fathers. Overall, though, there is warmth. We are both a little bit like orphans so this extended family swallows us up, and we accept this, happily, because it is a miracle when someone offers to hold your baby for five minutes so that you can eat.

Against this painted backdrop, we watch our children grow. We walk everywhere together. We know the topography of the village, its bends and curves, its tracks and private lanes, the hidden paths and shortcuts. There is a carved wooden owl at the end of one track in the woods near our home and we bless its head with our hands when we walk past, kicking the leaves as we go. I know the feeling of the smooth tarmac at one end of the village under my boots and the springy, neat grass on the cricket pitch, the gravel on the lanes and the pavement on the high street. A mile up the road and a mile backwards to our yellow door. Time to think.

At a baby group, I wear a white cotton Spanish-style dress and someone says, 'Is that national dress? Burmese?' 'No,' I say flatly, 'French Connection'. Then, often, 'Where are you from?' 'I'm from Hayes.' *Is this a game?* 'No, where are you *from?*' 'London.' It's a funny ritual, one I have known all of my life. So, I choose different answers for different situations. In Venice, I told one curious waiter that I was 'Egyptian', yes, since he had asked. This *is* a game. Then, in Paris, a complete stranger stopped me in a supermarket aisle near Les Invalides and asked if I was French Algerian. She also instructed me, gently, not to buy too many things from the patisserie. In Moldova, Eastern Europe, while visiting my step-sister, they exclaimed, 'Ah, she is one of us!' No, but thank you any way, '*Spasibo!*' In other parts of London, I can slip, a little, between Indian, Middle Eastern or Bangladeshi and I know just enough words to get me through polite niceties in a corner shop.

In Suffolk, in the medieval port and fishing village of Orford, we sat drinking hot chocolate from the Pump Street Bakery while a lovely family stared at me and my son for a few minutes before coming up to us and asking, with a little embarrassment at the directness of their question, if we were Israeli, for they were Dutch-Israeli on holiday. 'Our grandson looks just like your boy.' *Where are you from?* When answering such a question, there is always a pause, which, alas, grows longer, and longer, the more I age. There may come a time when I do not answer and simply smile. Yet, there is a small delight in borrowing these identities, for a moment, as people claim me as their own, as local, or familial, and that makes anyone feel less alone. My father had the look of an English gentleman with pale eyes and ruddy cheeks, but it was his accent which stood for an Anglo-Asian identity, and his brown hair, which remained dark and slicked with hair gel until the chemotherapy started.

Perhaps I need a map? We never had a geography class, but maps I know, I see those in films.

Where is Burma/Myanmar? It's on the telly: there's Michael Palin!

I have a child's atlas and glance at the multicoloured pages. I see that we are somewhere between India, Thailand and China. Going back was never an option for my parents, and never a reality in any sense because they had no money and, after all, it would not be the place they knew – their home had sunk into history and vanished like a sinkhole in time. I am the last child in our family to be raised in the ways of Anglo-Asian identity, colonial food and Burmese phrases, which I hear in the kitchen while my mother sips tea with my aunt. When my first son arrives, I realise we are the same and, finally, I do not feel alone. There are deep bloodlines which exist between us. All of our indigenous ancestors are summoned, resurrected, by his face; this, I sense, is how my father must have felt looking into the eyes of his firstborn: my almond-shaped eyes, a tuft of black hair and a nose, just like his. These thoughts haunt me now that he is gone, filling the corners of my world. Of course, this is the way of procreation, but it is more acutely felt when homesick, when lost, when one's family have all but disappeared, when the ghosts are thin on the ground, as it were. We named Inigo after Inigo Jones, who designed costumes and scenery for masques by Ben Jonson, and whose drawings I had seen in a programme for Shakespeare's *The Tempest*. We named him Lambert, after my father.

Inigo, which trees do these leaves belong to? Can you guess?

Under the great corridors of oaks (*Quercus robur*), an oaken gathering, in the centre of our village in Hampshire, giants and their shadows, dog-eared daffodils appear in spring. 'Witch's butter' and oakmoss cluster around the dead, fallen branches, which we study like illuminations of the Bible; my hands and fingers pressed into the great cracks in the bark, my wrist still aching from the weight of a child's rolling head, held during breastfeeding. Flying about the wood, insects swimming outwards, light around the sharp edges of this island of oaks. *Inigo, put your hand on the tree.* Children dawdle and shout behind tree trunks, dropping water bottles, crisp packets, dummies; their mothers push buggies out and into the damp tracks, disintegrating oak leaves in our pockets and earth, sandy and worm-strewn, slicked against our coats in a cloudless incantation of life as one child laughs and another howls atop a pile of leaves. I steal daffodils and put them in Inigo's hand. He likes to hold them in his buggy. In January, we hear wassailing, cups of ale spilt, knocking against each other, in this ancient ritual celebrated in the apple orchard.

We take Inigo, at around the age of three, to my aunt's house in Ealing and he sits at her table. She gives him a bowl of pork and cabbage, chicken curry, steamed rice and bread rolls. She pokes his ribs and they laugh. It is the last time she will cook for us. He knows her, he has met her several times before, but this will be the last time. By the winter she will have gone and I will be pregnant with

Orlando, our second son (after Woolf and Shakespeare). My father's brother, Lawrence, goes, too. Now all three siblings' lives retreat into history, into the folds in the rocks and the branches they climbed in Burma.

We make up stories inspired by the names of the cottages in the village like Bumblebee or Little Dovecote. Two children, now, growing under the oaks. This is an intermittently exhausting cycle of activity, but also a time of self-questioning and searching for answers which will fit the perfect shape that is the space between us, parent and child. I carry a small child from the oaks to our cottage, his legs awkwardly dangling from my hips, hands stretched around my neck. *Why don't you drive? (I don't want to).* Small children falling, walking, tripping, hopping, stumbling. My hands around their face, kissing them, we travel the lanes and pick up branches along the way, drag them, picking damsons and elders, sloes and blackberries. I still feel the fear of getting lost (an urban fear) and I trample out of the woods, quick, listening for the roads and the cars. Six whole years of this. It is a long song. An unending, sheltering summer which balances light and dark on the edge of a thimble.

Mothers meet across the many rows of oaks and when school starts we wave from either side of their perfectly formed lines, planted at these angles in 1805, not for landscaping purposes, but because they were once destined for shipbuilding. The shipbuilding never occurred and so they stand here, like nuns in silent prayer, stooped around a church and in an island of land. What do you call several, multiple rows of oaks? Is there a name for this constellation? An oaken matrix? Their leaves create a living carpet as deep as halfway up our boots in the autumn. I make work phone calls in their shade, parking my orange buggy near them, and pacing near a tree; I breastfeed both children on a bench beside them, wintry breath still in the air, freezing and tired.

I know the small strands of foliage which come to stand for little oak trees and I know the shape of acorns, 'fairy cups', which we collect in wonder. Dylan and I laugh at the fact we are still thriving, here, but nevertheless, each time I walk through this village, I know I am a long way from 'home'.

So, we make family our home. A family is a house, a family is a dwelling.

This is also true of music. My husband is a musician and our house is filled with instruments. I know his home is where the music is and it always has been; but we, too, are swept up in the daily ritual of practice, tuning and long, low notes on the trombone or piano lessons in the living room. I was never taught to play an instrument, except for a brief trial on the violin at my senior school. My father sang and occasionally whistled. Over and over, I sing to my children 'Silent Night' in our bathroom as they flick water over the tiles above the bathtub.

Thanks to Tracey Thorn's unearthing of these treasures, I hear the private, bittersweet songs of Molly Drake, the mother of the late folk singer, Nick Drake, on the radio. Molly and her son were both born in the same country as my father and her gentle, sorrowful lullabies, like 'How Wild the Wind Blows', connect me to a new and vivid sense of home. How strange it is to encounter these lost songs which she had written only for her children. We all listen to these songs together and I wonder if Molly and her family ever knew mine? At some point, they would have visited the same places, surely? Nick was born in 1948, eleven years after my father and while he was a toddler in Rangoon my father was entering adolescence and would soon commit that sinful act of eating the sacred mangoes from the Burmese monastery before being punished and exiled to Shalimar and Darjeeling.

Listening to Molly, I wonder which songs my own mother sang to me? Had her mother sung to her and did these lullabies take the form of folk songs from India and Burma? My mother cannot remember, she has grown too old and I cannot remember, either. One night, my husband and I go out and my mother sits downstairs while Inigo sleeps in his cot. We come home after an hour to find her singing to him as he stands in the cot fully awake, quiet, and watching my mother as she tries anything to get him to settle down. From the staircase and in the glow of a child's nightlight, I see the lower half of her body, her feet in slippers, swaying, and Inigo's bare feet standing in the cot. She is humming a melody I do not recognise. There are no words, only feelings attached to music deep within her.

A few years after Inigo's arrival, the second child's birth is a redemption, a revisionist retelling of the same story. After a few difficult moments, I am resting with a drip in my arm and happily looking at my phone, reading and doing a sudoku puzzle. A nurse comes into my hospital room and utters the golden sentence, 'Just a few hours and then I'll come back and you'll be ready to push.' My husband sleeps in a chair and we wait for Orlando. I imagine he will be a quiet child; he was born so gently, so easily. I go to bed with him in my arms, listening to the radio. I hear an announcement that the next elected President of the United States is Donald Trump. I blink in the news. Orlando sleeps and I retrace all the steps in my mind, all the things I did with Inigo, like a hymn sung again out loud, familiar, hands raised high and clapping out the rhythms in the darkness.

Months old and Orlando is a bull in a china shop, a gregarious smiler, social and as jovial as a cricket fan in sunglasses swigging from cans of lager at the Ashes, my husband proclaims. He throws everything from fruit to socks. We christen him 'the bowler', like my father. I look at the oaks and I see cricket bats now, licked with linseed oil. Everything is bowled, including my father's ceramic pheasant. He has enormous green eyes (Dylan's colour), but their shape is like mine, and pointy ears which eventually become half-hidden by light-brown curls.

Under the oaks, my second child learns to walk and balances on the once felled trees which lie like gnarled alligators across a patchwork of daffodils in spring. I have never before spent so long thinking about oak trees. I see them every day and we nod to each other. Or, rather, they bend their branches in sprung forms and I walk hooded, my right hand on the aluminium frame of the buggy (I am left-handed so my body naturally pivots from the right to the left, the muscles below my right shoulder and upper arm ache from the miles we walk). I wonder which ancient secrets lie inside their carcasses of splitting bark and creamy interiors, beetles scouring lines over burnt green fur and dew-crested webs. They have witnessed my history, as well as that of the entire village. These heavy, creaking scaffolds, filled with living organisms, are as alien to me as moondust, stars along the milky way. I knew the two apple trees from my childhood garden in Middlesex, but not these sweeping bodies of oak. I knew the height of an apple tree and the view from their pale, moss-silvery bark; I knew those, and I knew conifers (*leylandii*), as every suburban child does, a backdrop before a garden barbecue or a vacant set of swings, a deflating paddling pool abandoned in winter, or a child's stumpy, plastic slide. Oaks, they were bidden forth from Narnia. Or, in other mythologies, defend you against your enemies, as Susanna Clarke writes in her novel *Jonathan Strange & Mr Norrell*, fashioning doors into *faerie* land.

I tell my children about *fairie* doors. 'There's another,' I call out. Why not? I thrive on their joy. As a child, I had read the story of the Cottingley Fairies, in awe of the photographs these girls had seemed to produce, living proof of magic. There were images of fairies performing mesmerising *tableaux vivants* atop the trunk of a tree, a beech limb twisted and heavy against the lightness of their wings and delicate arms. The teenage Elsie and nine-year-old Frances had, of course, faked these images back in 1917, an audacious lie, pushing a little further the boundary between reality and fiction, the supernatural and the banal. In many ways, with their images of willowy trees and harebells, the Cottingley girls awoke something, perhaps a supernatural splendour nevertheless because they were tapping into the splintering distance between nature and the increasing drive towards the modern age of science and mechanical industry. So, they used this modernity against itself, the mechanical reproduction of the photographic image becoming a science which, in their hands, is magic. Their fairy images prompted not glittery, mawkish wonder, but renewed fascination with the natural world. It was nature's 'sleight of hand', ever present and yet unacknowledged, which was the very foundation for the girls' pictures. In Hampshire, almost a century later, we three Burmese children refuse our incorporation into myth, into Otherness and grab greedily at the things we can touch and make our mark on. Our reality is, surely, mysterious, *mysterical*, enough.

The oaks are majestic wonders: also, as the Woodland Trust professes on its website, *a national symbol of strength*. There could not be a more apt description of the way I feel about these oaks in the little village in Hampshire; they were constant and loyal, as sentries are, a physical reassurance of life when everything around me was uncertain, shifting and slipping out of reach. As a new mother, I felt safe inside this gathering, these corridors, planted in rows like a living library or ships' quarters (like the ships they were once destined to be). Solid, their physical strength grew as I grew, as a mother, stronger, quicker, unafraid. When the children could walk, we kicked leaves together and, all the while, through the stretch of the years, the physical sensation of our bodies mingled and vibrated, at some atom-shaped level, twinned with the movement of the trees. Our family gathered strength in our deep hibernation in this village. Enfolded. So, from here, a new knowledge.

Side by side,
my father's ghost and the Green Man,
and their songs in my throat make my grief and sorrow,
swallowed.

Ships

As a child, I had visited the *Mary Rose*, lost in 1545 and recovered in 1982, with my fellow classmates at school. We stood, it seemed, in the belly of a whale, her oaken bones appeared to breathe and perspire as the ship's remains were sprayed with water, and we stood inside these mists and watched the wood dampen, darken. We were led on to the viewing platform. Still, hushed as only small children can be, we felt the current of the sea and the pull of the tide as we stared into great planks of oak, bowing and stiffening in the air; we were not looking at a ship at all, we were transported to a different, uncanny state between earth and water, tree and air. It was a living thing and we were tiny and insignificant in its bellow's gill, its porous shadow. The *Mary Rose* remains the only ship I have ever entered and I am nearly in my fortieth year.

If you are to board a ship, you require a certain proficiency as a swimmer. I spent some of my school days at the top of a raked set of plastic seats gazing down at the line of the local swimming pool – its undulating contours visible from this height. When I was ten, my mother signed me up for lessons at Hayes Pool. My mother cannot swim and is afraid of water, hugging the sides of bridges each time she crosses them, which is unfortunate because she now lives in Exeter where all the water greets you at varying ends of the Exe.

At the Royal Museums Greenwich, I searched for evidence of my father's journey through archival records and photographs. Yet what interested me most was not the factual information, but the artwork, the paintings. I stood for a long time and imagined the noises of departure in one particular painting. I was more familiar with the rhythms of walking, the sounds which led me through the woods in Hampshire and Hurtwood's cathedral of trees in Peaslake; I knew the sound of the train to London, my father's Ford Escort along the Uxbridge Road and the 140 bus to Heathrow.

In *The Parting Cheer* by Henry Nelson O'Neil, painted in 1862, we see groups of people gathered at the quayside as an emigrant ship departs. In the lower bottom corner is a mother with her two children, one at her knees and another outstretched and asleep on her lap. We see the velvet, muddied folds of her skirt which drapes half of her body, crimson, and then the line of her arm as she rests her face on a cupped hand. While others wave handkerchiefs, hats and arms, she is subdued, bored even, weary of this sight.

'She may be the wife of one of the departing sailors,' the Royal Museums Greenwich speculates on its website, 'who, deprived of support, is left alone with two small children. Her plight is emphasised by the child's muddy skirt, imploring eyes and the abandoned stance of the younger sleeping child.'

This female figure is marginal, literally, on the edge of the painting, as are her children. The title of the painting might refer to a 'cheer', a goodbye, but stories such as this woman's often remain silent. The catalogue listing refers to the 'emigrants' sailing to North America with the Thames shown as 'an industrial landscape, with smoking chimneys and a forest of ships' masts' and I find myself thinking about my father here, waving goodbye, but also the women in my family, fastened to the shore, like my great-grandmothers whom I have never met. They remained behind, while their grown-up children sailed to England.

Who did you wave goodbye to?

My father travelled by ship to Southampton, England, in the mid-1950s, still a boyish eighteen years of age and sent on ahead, before his sister and his parents, setting sail on a voyage to join his elder brother, Lawrence, in Essex. Lawrence had already found employment with the British Bata Shoe company in East Tilbury, Essex, and there was a job for my father awaiting him on arrival in England. On the way, he travelled via Egypt and ate honey-soaked dates. I imagine him in a minor role in Agatha Christie's *Death on the Nile*, sitting somewhere beneath whirling ceiling fans, a kid smoking on the decks. At some point, he decides to get some tattoos. He wants blue swallows on his right arm, in memory of the sailors he meets. Then, an English rose because England is the place he hopes to call home.

There is a small photograph of my father's belongings on board the ship before he left. Wrapped like a Christmas stocking, there is an L-shaped package, around a metre in length: letters, parcels, hidden tobacco, his 'shark skin' (finely woven) suit, tennis shoes, a cricket bat, passport and the tiny carved figures which were once pressed into his young hands by prisoners of war. After he arrived in England he never visited a single other country and he never once set foot on a ship again, not even a pleasure cruiser down the Thames. The irony is that many parcels were also sent back to Burma by my aunt, but she tells me, many times, and with great sadness, that not one was received by those left behind, returned to sender or simply destroyed.

Inevitably, my father played poker with the other boys below the decks and gambled away his First Class ticket, bought by his sister's husband, Hugh, who loved him dearly. My father spent the rest of the journey exploring the various milieus within that crowded ship and, possibly, listening to sport on the radio. He was used to being a boarder and probably coped well on the ship, but I'm sure he felt different, uneasy, the more time he spent away from everything he had once known. Everything was lost in limbo on board the ship to England; my father was adrift, floating between a childhood in India and an adulthood in London, caught in a voluminous cloud of unknown, ambiguous potential, past and future, man and child. He also carried with him the ghosts which haunted him further, into adulthood: the prisoners of war, the boys who drowned in the boating accident at school, friends and neighbours who did not survive the war, his great-grandfather, great-grandmother, his pet dogs and the living flora and fauna of India such as the Oriole and Jacana birds, which he must have seen at the harbour spreading their wings for the last time.

Ships are at the centre of the migrant's story, the immigrant experience, as one path is closed and another taken, a journey which alters the timelines and slowly carves new spaces in the imagination of the traveller. Each morning, for almost a decade, I had passed the rows of oaks in my Hampshire village and contemplated their original purpose as the timber for ships which would set sail from Portsmouth or Southampton at the turn of the nineteenth century; I imagined the ships which brought my family here and rooted us in England, but somehow they remained in an oneiric realm.

Storm-wracked, sun-bleached, a ship occupies a sphere of human existence determined by the elements, at the mercy of the wind and the shape of the sun, the current of water and the weight of invisible things. Voyages test systems of belief. Indeed, Raimond's father had his tarot cards read, before he boarded the *SS Hersey*. Ships operate along the boundaries between animal and mineral, water, air, earth and fire. The very notion of floating, albeit within a body of water, is akin to a kind of mysticism. Levitation requires a current of air below one's body, so let's call the act of sailing a form of dreaming: wandering, wondering, floating. Here, a body of water is a *séance*-site.

Can ghosts breathe? The night swallows my father whole, so he listens to the bowels of the ship and puts his hand on the floor of the deck, steadying himself. The prisoners of war come first, bearing more gifts for him, little pieces of carved bone splintering from the hollows of their palms. Then, the boys who drowned in the river come back to him. The ruffled Irish beard of his paternal, great-grandfather. His Burmese grandmother's long hair, stretched across three chairs made of teak in her home in Mogok. Does he have a ruby in his pocket, too? A 'pigeon's blood' stone, it rolls sideways, it spreads uneven light across polished oak beams and whitewashed walls. Back on land, a tiger is glimpsed, an orange flame beneath the hills in Darjeeling. A child who looks just like my father waves from the harbour. Then, the child turns his back. The smooth back of his head and the silhouette of the city. The stars and sloping clouds, purpling shades of an Indian sky are falling behind my father's left ear, disappearing, in granular time, over the hills. The shape of his grandmother's black hair draped over the backs of three chairs.

Now this book, my words, are a ship. A book derives its matter from a tree, does it not? And, so does a ship's frame, does it not? But this book is not my ship, it is my father's, carrying my family safely within it, through all of the little gaps in space and time. I am turning the world sideways and the moon and the sun have retreated. We inhabit a gap in time. Am I closing this gap, or am I jamming it open? Perhaps I am saying goodbye. Because I had to be prompted to kiss my father's body after he died and, of course, I do not believe my aunt has gone. In some other dimension of the universe, my aunt is still in her kitchen, making oxtail soup and moving slowly towards the kettle and the knife on the wall. What if I don't want to say goodbye? But they are already leaving me.

A single tarot card on the decks of a ship. It drops. It lands.

A red-hooded woman with black hair is holding a chalice by a river.

The Five of Cups. Disappointment. Sorrow.

Another card. It is The Seer. A woman in a blue cape and crimson gown on a throne.

She is surrounded by the sea. Water flows around her: Life.

Everything must go back to the sea.

First, a tidal wave.

My aunt's kitchen is flooded with water and the china tea cups with pictures of dogs or English flowers, bob up and down, the plastic tablecloth with ivy wreaths unfurls and spreads like a raft; Constable's *The Hay Wain* somersaults near the door frame and is submerged by the weight of her brown glazed teapot. Beyond this vitrine, the severed heads of two 'exotics', two Indian men made of plaster and turbaned, smiling widely, are freed from their mantle on the golden embossed wallpaper; rectangular moons – her hallway lights, shiver above the tidelines, golden wallpaper flapping against the door. The telephone is intermittently ringing, burbling, in the hallway, deep, underwater, and its cord, a rubber algology. A microscopic whale song. The frosted glass on my aunt's inner door, in the porch, is loosened and water spills out into the avenue, under the cherry blossom. Foamy, milky drifts of rice spilling from open jars, margarine tubs open like neon oysters.

In Hayes, the living room is tipped sideways and the flood defences burst on the Grand Union Canal. Wedged between two armchairs and a nest of tables, the sink in the kitchen has erupted into a Grecian water fountain. My father's blue cigarette lighter is navigating huge waves, riding their crest as sodden, bent cigarettes touch the seabed, the parquet floor. Old Holborn tobacco forms a knot of auburn seaweed near a door handle. Photographs in silver frames from Argos are like razor clams cutting across the axis of the water; bookies' slips and several five-pound notes transform into mermaids' purses and my father's car keys are like spider crabs in silvery armour. Our net curtains make diaphanous shapes in the water and the television, split open, reveals a sunken treasure of silken petals from my mother's vase – a shoal of rose-coloured fish. My father's denim jeans and 'gum boots' are caught in a whirlpool, clogging and spluttering out great bubbles of air, old bits of grass dislodging from the soles of the boots. My wedding dress, with its layers of duchess satin and silk, fan out like a mermaid's tail and flick over and over, over and over. The water reaches the ceiling and my father's grey-rimmed glasses spin around the light fittings like electric eels.

In Peaslake, our cuckoo clock from the Black Forest in Germany strikes and the water pumps in through the floorboards. The beech trees fold and collapse. Water rises from the road and subsumes our terrace. Bricks loosen. Bird feeders and cricket bats dance in the silent flood. Plant pots and a garden statue in the shape of a figure from the Terracotta Army juts forwards and bumps against the wheel of Dylan's Nissan Micra, now almost vertical and the water keeps coming. Bicycles of all shapes and sizes tangle into an ungainly wreck, spokes turning, mud loosening all around. Inky explosions of oil and dirty rainwater from outside tanks and water butts. Something is alight, momentarily, before it plunges into the darkness of the river which has now consumed everything. The hills are islands, deep in water, floodplains all around; ash and beech trees in this swimming pool, the owls resting atop their branches. The Hooghly River in India enters into burbling dialogue with the River Tillingborne.

In Hampshire, the oaks have fallen, but they are not oaks anymore. Zig-zagging along the River Test, they are a fleet of ships with their sails up, soaring, entering a flooded high street and navigating the wreckage of shop signs and litter bins, a ladybird carved from wood and beer barrels like lobster pots. A medusa's head of branches with strands of ivy and cow parsley twists around the ships and gently nudges their bows. A dog's lead and a buggy, like driftwood, enter the path of the ships and then disappear beneath the waves. The moon shines against the sails and their billowing forms breathe in soft rhythms against a black sky. Drenched strands of green and violet *Verbena bonariensis* float up from sunken gardens and meet, tip to tip, tendril to tendril, with school ties and the laces of trainers like Michelangelo's *Creation of Adam* in the Sistine Chapel. Seven kinds of lavender spill across our yellow front door, *Vermeer* yellow, and the letterbox chatters with sloe berries, blue and vermillion.

Then, an empty space. Ossified time. My heart is like an ammonite.

The hourglass turns.

Storm-wracked, like Prospero and Miranda, I am left with these words, with you, father, and this book, this *ship-wracked, ship-shaped* book. Were they, too, not newly made immigrants on their isle?

We began with a map. Where are the maps?

I can linger here, a little while longer, with Sycorax the witch, for the spells are cast, the ghosts are freed. In a hooded dress, she rests her palms flat on my aunt's table and stares blankly at me with black eyes. I can wait here, but you must return to the boy on the shoreline. The missing child. The thief. 'Poker'. Beloved son and beloved friend. Look for the hills shaped like your grandmother's hair across three teak chairs. Look for the birds, the bulbuls, and listen to their calling. See the flare of the tiger's movement in the jungle and wait for its breath by your ear. Be free and do not cry. You were meant to go back, but you never did. Go. I have no regret in this. You are relinquished.

I have no sorrow. Roll up your sleeves. Go back to the water. On your back are your things, a pack of cards and the keys to your sister's house in Shalimar. *Shalimar.* Do you remember? Your scratch-haired dog is waiting and they have rolled back the chairs on the veranda.

The boy has half turned to face me on the shoreline. His face appears and I know it. It is my son, Inigo.

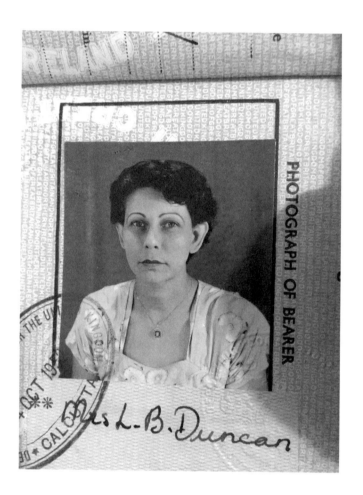

PHOTOGRAPH OF BEARER

Mrs L. B. Duncan

III

Tracks

Devon, rivers

Water can wear away even the hardest rock.

BURMESE PROVERB

I feel, no more, the pebble which turned once in my chest ten years ago.

The three of us, myself and my two children, walk to the flaking, lime and loam-walled barns with their crumbling sheets of plaster and exposed beam, and enter the half-shadow of a shepherd's makeshift shelter for lambs and their mothers as winter falls. Hay is strewn and clags the ground, sweet and sulphurous, earthen. It is 4.30 p.m. and the geese fly over our heads each day in the cold unbroken light. My knuckles are pink and I have carried a mug of hot tea down here. My boys are on their scooters. The wheels enter the split and curdled mud, dragged to the periphery of the barn. Inside, some newborn lambs are fed by bottle. My lambs are here, I think to myself. They are grown, no longer carried.

The old shepherd and I talk about the simple nature of this process and its honesty; a shepherd's job is to protect these lambs and to nourish them. This, this work, takes all night and all day, in sporadic shifts, out into the field to check pregnant ewes. 1 a.m. 4 a.m. Out into the field. The shepherd's lights dazzle even the owls. I lie awake facing a square of moonlight reflected on a wall. I check the clock on my phone. *The cricket, Dad, India versus Pakistan.* A lamb calls out in the bank of a meadow. In the morning, a whiteness bleeds through an open sky and the ash trees are very still.

I am new to these parts. The view has remained unchanged for hundreds of years: a hamlet with several houses, a mansion, fields on either side and then further and all around, no main road and no modern developments. A little Saxon church in a flooded field in December. I count the elder trees, the rosehips, so perfect, and the trodden nettles, the remains of wild strawberries and the holly, evergreen against the husks of lavender.

I find our house on an enlarged Ordnance Survey map printed on the walls of the visitor centre at Killerton, an eighteenth-century property owned by the National Trust, painted pink and surrounded by rolling hills and parkland. My finger touches the tiny square on the wall which represents our home in Devon, nestled amongst the villages of Brampford Speke, Thorverton, Columbjohn and Silverton. I have this map at home, purchased before we even bought the house, and I have folded out its pages many times since. I stare at the vivid shape of the land, the pale-blue lines (the River Exe and the River Culm), tiny green trees (Killerton Park, Stoke Hill, Ashclyst Forest, White Down Copse and Paradise Copse) and incongruous shapes (mills, farms and forts), but my eyes follow, more closely, the long strands of pink diamonds like Christmas lights, which mark out the public footpaths to Exeter (10 miles) and Tiverton (15 miles). All of these hieroglyphs never fail to excite me as my consciousness takes on the form of a swift flying over the fields, or a raven in the clouds.

On the ground, we have four russet apple trees and a damson, but better still, we have vines which sweep across the front of the house. The day before we move in, we know the house is empty so we walk up to the wooden gate and discover these grapes. I hear for the first time the breeze through the large willow tree which looms over our garden. It is this sound which emphasises how quiet it is, this slow gush, a breath, which stirs through its branches and tiny leaves, gently announcing itself and ornamenting the peace.

It is the sound of our new home.

Our daylight rhythms and daily routines, walking to school, walking back, intersect with those of the old shepherd's ways. His sheepdogs curl around us, herding us as they do the sheep.

(every time we meet)

Is that your real hair colour? It's very black.

Yes.

You'se dye that, for sure.

(smiling) No, I don't! (not yet...)

Well, I wish I had hair dark like that, mine's all grey...

One afternoon, we discover him tending a lame creature, kicked by its mother in the dark. It happens like this, sometimes. The lamb is inside the 'shoulder' of the barn, near the outer recesses which house sick animals. Front legs folded underneath its body and warmed by fresh hay, the lamb turns and raises its head as we move closer. The children are throwing new hay from wrapped bales into the courtyard of the barn, another area which houses at least fifty pregnant ewes. I lean into the 'cubicle' where the lame animal sits, its eyes darting about, lively despite its injury. I pick up this lamb and his head is dipped, tucked under my arms, glad of the warmth. My hands against his rib cage. How softly this one comes into my arms, still a little blood on his back, a tongue and saliva on my hands. *Stop it now, stop throwing the hay,* I call out. My voice is only an echo in this Bethlehem, a shelter full of ancient noise. My exile's heart is fastened to these creatures, kinfolk, now, on the River Exe.

And this is how things start, again. It is a conversation between two old worlds: my father's world which I carry with me and the shepherd's world which is all of four miles square, the farmland. My father kept a goat at his boarding school, but never a lamb. It was a tradition I never understood. Yet, so it is that I have entered into my aunt's Constable painting. I am in rural Devon, between Exmoor and Dartmoor, in a valley, flat and fielded. Step out into the lane and there are fields of wheat. Step out into the fields and there are cows and sheep. The river is a short walk away. I make a mental note: I am almost certain that I am the first woman of Anglo-Asian heritage to call this hamlet in Devon my home. This is a border crossing, an enchantment, splitting open a gap between Devon and my father's homelands in India and Burma.

A few days after we arrive here, I decide to take the children for an extended walk and we follow the map out to Killerton. We walk to the main road and then it is a direct path all the way to the part marked on the map as 'the enclosure'. With a bike and a buggy, we trek down in the sunlight, climbing embankments and trenches each time a tractor or lorry passes. The children are full of questions. 'Where are we going?', 'Can we get an ice cream?', 'Are there bulls?' There are no bulls, but we do pass a rare-breed farm and end up on a track which passes through deep rivers of mud and the archaic stench of soiled hay. We enter the estate via a footpath and we stumble down the land from the 'wrong' side of a fence, the place outside of the public periphery of the estate. *What does this mean?* I think I like this indirection, this subversion of routes. Finally, we reach the main visitor centre and buy those ice creams, which could not have come soon enough after almost two hours of walking with a small child and a baby in a buggy.

In the early autumn, we find a perfect sparrows' nest in the hedgerow. 'Put it back,' Inigo says. We pick sloe berries, standing on a chair carried from our kitchen. I roll up my dress and save them in my pockets. I watch the colours of the valley alter with the light, the sun kissing their dense shapes. Lichen grows all over a neighbour's dead tree and I wander in between its outstretched branches; a sleeping, fallen ash tree which hides rare lichen. I see two women dressed in what can only be described as 'country attire', whispering near another ash over by the field just a few hundred metres north of our house. They lean into its hollow. *What could they be saying?* They appear to me as if they are standing over a sleeping baby in a crib. Moving closer, I say hello and they tell me, quietly, that they are geographers from the university and that the lichen is what they study. They stand and examine the split interior and its flowering moss which is brilliant green, egg-wash yellow and cloud-shaped. I pinch the surface of the bark of the tree and it feels springy, dense. It holds a reservoir of secrets. We talk for a long time by the ash, a casual communion, but despite always looking out for them, I never see these women again.

It has been a decade since my father's death and we find ourselves in this small hamlet in the Exe Valley. When you come to know a place such as this, you listen to it first, and then you know its name. We walk a circular route around the farmland and listen to swifts, starlings and sparrows. We watch swallows and chaffinches, robins and seagulls picking out worms from the newly dug earth, arriving in a collective movement on the soil. The wings of the seagulls are like white envelopes being opened over the red Devon fields.

I watch the wind in the wheat fields. There is a particular way in which the wind moves through such open, sparse terrain, echoing through the valley. I listen to the metal cattle grids and the gates, a yawning, opening and closing. There is also the sound of the wind when it batters our chimneys at the top of the house and sends a torrent of noise down its blank recesses. The noise is so loud I think the chimney stacks may fall down. At night, I grip my pillow when I hear the wind shuttle through the fireplace. One singular flowerpot seems to roll about and knock an exterior wall during a storm. The old ceramic flowerpot makes the same 'knock, knock-d-d-d-d-d' all through the night. Neither of us go out to move it, or nudge it out of the way of the wall.

When summer comes, there is the noise of water being sprayed over the crops, a hiss and gulp, a sizzling sound, which takes a while to recognise and learn. We stare out from our windows upstairs and search for the sounds. We count them. By our third year in this house, we shall not only know each sound and be able to name each thing we hear, but also expect them at different times of the day, unconsciously rooting ourselves in this sense of place. We hear the A396 between Rewe and Stoke Canon, while rollers flatten the fields, rattling along the ground. We hear a hedge cutter, the sound of lorries carrying grain, cattle being moved in large cattle transporters.

In the distance, the train between London and Exeter swims past our bedroom window, lights momentarily dotting the horizon, and each time I think of the artery it provides into Paddington, the station that always took me home from university to Hayes. My six-year-old son watches the train, silenced, every time. *Look, there it is, the train!* Between brief domestic discussions and minor quarrels, we stop ourselves and wait for it to pass, far off, far beyond the two large fields north of our house. A literal 'train' of thought in the air. I return a large plate to the table. My youngest son comes in and asks for a glass of water. His mouth misses the glass and it spills.

In between writing of all kinds, I travel to London to teach at a university and I also begin working at a school, which I grow to love for its routines and smiling faces, even when it is very early in the morning and bitterly cold. I keep walking past a building with the name 'Ondaatje' etched into stone. My tiredness means that I think very little about this 'Ondaatje' shaped message until one day I acknowledge its meaning. No, not Michael, but his brother, Christopher, was educated here many years ago. My father went to school against the backdrop of the Himalayan mountain range and now I am at a school which sits at the bottom of a very different hillside. Of course, that famous surname was also there when I worked at the National Gallery and often strolled over to its sibling, the National Portrait Gallery, where a part of the building bears the name, the 'Ondaatje Wing'. Full circle, I am here, carrying still within me the rhythm of words I had first read while travelling on a bus to Ealing in my teenage years. Perhaps Michael, a post-colonial kid of the same generation as my father, more or less, would find amusement in how things have worked out; their ships from another continent pass into the pages of this book. Inevitably, someone places a bet.

Who will win the cricket this year?

In January, we walk to the river and the children drag large, sprawling entities, tree branches, along the riverbank. They wield them high above their heads, kneel and examine them, scratch their surfaces. The river is low here, on this side of Exeter, and the current is steady. We slide past fences and 'kissing gates', avoiding cattle and fields of fodder beet and kale, the air stinging with the rich smell of green-leafed brassicas, pungent and bitter. The whole affair is dirty, thorny, stinking and frost-bitten. Electricity pylons appear staked to the ground like triffids in this rural, open-skied place. A tall church spire beyond the hills is like a Byzantine relic. While we walk along the River Exe, the curves of time ripple backwards and my father is there, sitting by the Irrawaddy River in Burma. He passes his hands through the bullrushes. Sometimes, he spies a dolphin.

Further, near the river and deep into the valley, crosswinds beat against our faces like taut elastic bands and the fields sing a low, continuous lyric. A vowel in the mouth, no, in the *throat* of the valley. OoOoo...OoOoo. High-pitch frequencies. I imagine visible wavelengths the colour of red soil and bubbling flotsam on the riverbank. The children are drawn to where water collects and pools, low and sharp inclines on the roads, which they can skid through, and the corners of our garden which they naturally turn into dens and faery gardens (a tree stump in a patch of grass). A bird flies into our porch and I catch it. *My mother's hands moving birds from the aviary.*

We listen to the borders between the brick and briar, telegraph poles and internet wires, the asphalt and the cobble. We find a dawdling dandelion weed, crestfallen between pavement and gutter; a wild meadow in a city park; a feather in a bottle, sea-glass fashioned into earrings at the market, copper-coloured lichen on the rooftops of old sheds, water muttering in the canals by the suburbs. We hang all of these things on a line of memory and an enchantment, a song, as we walk home from our bus stop.

We also listen to each other. Occasionally, my eldest son speaks with an unfamiliar cadence, a longer emphasis on some vowels or consonants, and I turn to him and listen more intently. Inigo never met my father, yet my husband says, 'He sounds like your family.' Perhaps he has absorbed some of my mother's intonation, her accented English. I must admit, it takes me a long time before I realise that the sound I hear bears the exilic rhyme of my own voice, an echo which reaches me, oddly, out of nowhere. Residual traces of once colonised voices, now colonise my own child's body, as they had mine. Inherited histories of trauma loosen and become friable, mutable, the more we travel along these lines of power and reclaim body and mind. Over time, this colonisation of the body, engendered through DNA, comes to represent a more tender geography and our lineal likeness, as it finds its way to the surface of the present, is a map of the power we hold inside ourselves.

Which parts of my body belong to my indigenous heritage? Often, my father would hold my arm up and ask me to turn it so that my elbow faced upwards. I have a small dimple there, above my elbow. 'There it is, my mother's arm was the same.' My chin is like his, too, and my nose. I have my mother's hair and eyebrows. I turn my arms over and place my fingers on the dimple on the crease above my elbow. Which parts of my body were mine alone? Which characteristics did I originate? Was everything, even my fingernails, truly an inheritance? The study of genetics tells me this is so, but what if our environments change us, also, irrevocably, in visible and invisible ways? Over time, every living thing adapts to its habitat. What, then, is the nature of my heartwood self?

What about other kinds of transformations which exist beyond the biological, the genealogical? Is not the body-mind multiple? How are these changes marked in time in the bodies of our future selves, like the differing wood on the rings of a tree? In her essay on dendrochronology, the dating of trees, Jessica J Lee observes the varying colours of wood inside a tree, noticing how 'the scars of a heart shake cut across its inner rings (…) a marker of transformation'. How were my own familial scars and transformations, from generation to generation, mapped out? For trees, duration grows out in pools of movement, but they also register the past in every new gesture of life. Time, then, is a circular experience. Duration passes as a cyclical movement, a spinning, a rotation. Growth makes itself apparent in the shape of a circle. A forest of trees, then, represents time on a horizontal level, as well as the vertical. Not only this, but time is intensified at various points, older trees mingling with the saplings. Time is a circular symphony, so I twirl around and around, and my children, too, as they gather up the hoops, the loops, of my father's dance. Under the mango trees in Rangoon, he danced, and we followed.

In the present, my son's voice makes the sound of a Devonian whisper in his body, which is also an exilic instrument, in an island hundreds of years and miles away from its first utterance within a tribal community in the forested regions of Burma.

We find much joy out in Devon, but there are also further struggles. For that is the way of all life, is it not? Out of the blue, my youngest child, Orlando, starts to experience febrile seizures. Until now, I had thought myself to be a fearless protector. I was never ill as a child and they were the same, I had thought, strong like their mother. How foolish I was to ever believe that.

Barbara Hepworth's *Infant*, a sculpture of her son Paul, carved from Burmese wood, seems to haunt me. When I first saw Hepworth's sculpture, I said aloud, again and again, '*I* have a Burmese baby. *I, too,* have a Burmese baby.' He lives in St Ives, in the land of my husband's ancestors. He lived there long before my babies came.

We go through seizure after seizure, near-misses, slightly raised temperatures, me growing ever more watchful as these fits take hold. Would I rather Orlando was this baby's twin, momentarily caught in the shape of a wooden statue?

He sleeps. His soft cheeks are touching the folds of the blue bedsheet.

His mouth opens. A half syllable escapes his lips. A hum. A breath. A breath. A foot bends and an arm taps against the sides of his white wooden cot. Hollow, pinewood notes in the night. A breath. A breath. A fingernail buried in a knot of hair. Curls gathered behind his ears. Like this, he falls fast into the furnace. White coals at his cheeks.

A breath. A breath. A breath.

Electric pulse through his arms and another at his neck. I carry him into our bed and still, he jolts. A silent spell.

He is claimed, again, by the night, as I watch my baby

disappear behind his own eyelids, falling into the cracks of heat and snaking waves of lightning. 'Wake up', I say, softly, but he is still being pulled through the wires, through the tunnels of movement. My fast, flat palm on his forehead. My heart in my mouth. We check for signs as we pick up the phone from the bed and make the call. My husband opens the gate outside and looks for the blue lights across the fields.

He is a note of music caught jangling sideways, stuttering. A piano key which won't come loose. D-d-dddd-dddd. D-d-d-d-d. Then, I am left with this changeling on the bed; an enchanted thing which I cannot interrupt, nor quieten. Little breaths, I am searching, listening in the black for the little breaths. I hold my own breath, for I cannot hear him. I hold my own breath, but the changeling is now passing silently into the fold.

A febrile seizure is a thousand alarm bells after midnight. I am not even a witness, nor guard. I am exiled from my baby's world, and he from mine.

Hepworth carved a Burmese Baby from the blackest wood, silent and shining. She conjured him with her own hands. Oval-faced and oval-bodied. Sleeping. His head is fixed in a perpetual shifting towards an invisible pillow, nested in his upheld arms above. No longer swaddled deep within the grain of the mother tree. He is ever more rounded in the light which enters from her Cornish garden.

While my baby shakes in the night, her baby is ever so still, still, still, like the Burmese tree he was born from. His heartbeat can never stop. His breaths were never taken. He holds the spirit of the element which shaped him, the current of the wind and the moonlight. He is caught in time. No, he understands only the cadence of light and shadow, curve and form. Time, for him, is irrelevant because he will always be *her* wooden baby. Such tenderness in that gesture. His cheek a perfect reflection of her love. But he is not *mine*.

My baby is on the bed and I am waiting in the dark. I do not want my baby to be a copy, though they are twins. I hold my right hand against his chest while my other hand brushes his curls away from his wet face.

'I do not want your Burmese baby,' I seem to say out loud. 'I do not want him to turn into the teak tree, though this spell is breaking us. I want my baby. I want my baby. I will give you my hand, my cheek, for your forest, if you return my child. I will come away with you. I will accept the binding. Please pass him back through the fold.'

Then the deal is struck.

He travels through the clouds behind his eyelids and opens his large green eyes, whose pools of light I inspect for signs of a muted forest, another gathering fever. His movements are now ordinary, earth-bound, human. Blinking. Sniffing. Yawning. A slow unfurling of a pointed finger or a wrinkling of his nose. A smile. A grimace. A hundred different emotions which speak only of a child's restless nature. His head against my chest. His hand in my hand. He drinks water and we sit up on the bed, on the damp sheets, on the pillows. Sleep arrives quickly for him. But I am awake, staring out at the stars.

Elsewhere, incense burns the colour of Burmese wood. A flame is dampened. Maggie, my half-Shan grandmother, is fanning smoke at the foot of the twelfth-century Temples of Indein on the West Bank of Inle Lake. Spinning clusters of crumbling orange brick ascend from a veil of green leaves. The foliage spreads and burrows deep beneath Maggie's feet.

Orlando passes the age where seizures are most common and he is completely well again. But I still check his temperature at night, especially in the heat of the summer. I keep a tray of ice cubes in the fridge and I crush them in my mouth before passing them to him, a habit we have kept up as the years go by. Now, he asks for ice cubes whenever he is hot.

When our first July approaches in the house in Devon, I take my camera phone and I film Inigo darting through barley fields under thunderous skies, laughing and yelling, half spooked, as the echoes send tiny shockwaves across the vibrating tips of the tall grasses. Wild laughter which spills over into shrieks and roars. We part the barley as we run. A swallow in the sky. We lose each other and call out again. A chasm of sound which drops off into nothingness. We find each other and run back. We criss-cross each other, while the barley enfolds itself around us until the edge of the field seems far away. The parting of the barley like a fan shivering open. Have you ever seen a barley field and stood inside its stadium of movement? Still, I do not yet know this current of air and soil which engenders river and ground. We greet each other, as the shepherd greets me, and we begin a conversation.

Where did this Burmese baby come from and how does he meet me in the barley, after all these years alone, the only Burmese child? I find him, I find him. We find each other. My aunt's wide hands and the smell of her perfume at her wrists, *Samsara*, is coursing through the barley. My father's smoke from his Old Holborn roll-ups simmers in the Earth. My mother stands at the gate of our house, afraid of the wilderness, though she, too, like my father and his sister, was born where the rice fields were harvested and the river rose in winter. The River Exe spills over into the fields in Devon and my father's ghost lingers near the waterlogged lanes; he describes to me the taste of snow from Kanchenjunga.

Look! A river and a wheat field in Devon. A twitching robin on the wheelbarrow, a rain-soaked pine cone on the grass, its colour deepening.

After all is said and done, we are a just a family of tigers roaring at the Green Man.

An opening

Small gestures. The weight of the bird in our porch. The weight of the bird missing my cupped hands. A skylight. Flight. A child's hand steadies the old brass bell inside our porch. Then, something else breaks the flow of water. We loop back on ourselves.

The garage door slides backwards and reveals a rectangular-shaped view, a cinema screen, through which to view the world. It is a still image. The lane and the fields beyond. A scooter by our gate. I step back into the shade of the garage and watch the world play itself over and over; I have carried books into and out of this space and crept amongst the boxes we have never properly unpacked. An old fireplace screen in the shape of a brass peacock, a set of paintbrushes, a broken silver buggy and a lawnmower are the audience in this theatre.

On the radio, we hear old words in new contexts: 'lockdown', 'self-isolation', 'virus'. The children are sent home and we work with them in makeshift places, at the kitchen table or on the floor by the sofa. This could be a closing down of life, an ellipsis, an empty space between a paragraph or an unchartered island, but of course those things are never truly empty, they are an opening, not a closing-off, unmarked: the space between a paragraph is where all the thinking takes place. So that is what we all do, but especially me. This is where I write this book. In the unmarked places, the locked-down zone, this other world opens up to me.

The tension inside needs to dissolve, so we skip schoolwork and we walk. I take only Inigo. We see folds of green silken leaves, wild garlic up at the river's edge. We tear it from its roots and roll it, filling our pockets. Here,

I see my aunt's hands on a chopping board. Garlic in her prawn curry, pounded cardamom and sweet ginger on his fingertips. 'Do you remember her curry, Inigo? You tasted it when you were one.' When you enter this cool riverbank, you smell the leaves first and then you see it, like 'blinded' daffodils (without their flowers), their flowers absent in spring. Sweet and stinging on your tongue.

Sheltering, from what I don't know, I take refuge in the garage and rummage around in boxes, some still holding remnants from previous house moves, all the way back to our move from Surrey to Berkshire, or from Berkshire to Hampshire. After many years, I locate the sari we bought in Southall; my brilliant gift from Dylan, bought on my twenty-first birthday. I pull it over my legs and walk out into the garden, a mermaid's tail. I tie the long lengths of silk which form the scarf (*chuni*) to an apple tree, its deep pink buds still tightly bound. Flaps of red fabric bruise the sky and ripple across a backdrop of clouds and branches. Glittery, golden shapes weigh heavy on the tree and hang in folds. The fabric is caught in a vortex, an invisible chasm. *How do you film the wind?*

On Easter Sunday, a neighbour gently rests a plate on our doorstep: four freshly baked cinnamon buns. Easter bells toll across the fields from the Saxon church. In the afternoon it seems only right to walk to a church, but instead we discover the ruins of an old farmhouse. Crosswinds, fierce and freezing, send shockwaves of movement over the long grass. Several colours of lichen, green and orange on the stones. My hand trying to catch the current of air amongst the gravestones. Children giddy and screaming as they run between the hedgerows. I stand by the doorway of the church.

On the way home from the walk I take each day with Orlando in his buggy (fifty minutes across farmland and then a main road), leaving Dylan with Inigo doing equations and fractions, speaking to teachers on a computer screen, their faces like spirits from a distant past, I linger near a window. Shadows from the beech trees outside pass over the frame. Each movement is different, tracing branches across squares of light. It is 4 p.m. and I cannot move. I concentrate on these arboreal shapes. Inside outside, outside inside. All of time is askew in these hours before night. My mother is passing clothes from the washing line to me in our garden in Hayes. I am running along our garden path while my father collects leaves. Back in the present, Orlando holds a brightly coloured sweet wrapper in his hand and it is swept up in the wind. Perhaps my father will catch it, his invisible hands moving in the sky above us. *Orlando, don't run too fast! Wait for me.*

Round and round we go. Performing daily domestic rituals, intensified in this locked-down state, shared between us but nevertheless unending, I seem to have the time to notice how my husband's cobalt-blue V-neck jumper has come undone with a tear around the neckline, useless after just one week. I take its blue-black collar and feel the wool between my fingers. It feels thin. The label bears the word 'Myanmar'; Burmese factory workers have made this item of clothing and it finds its way into my hands, tiny threads of physical connection and cultural meaning which strike me like a blow to the ribs. Production costs are evidently so low that the seams untangle easily. I have rarely met any other Burmese people. To find this piece of manufactured clothing in my hands and know that it was once held by a fellow Burman is at once exciting and devasting – *how much were they paid and how many days would they have to work to buy this item back from the factory they have laboured in?* The shops are closed in 'lockdown', so I take out a needle and thread. As I do this, I realise I am forced to reckon with the fact that I am Burmese and my Anglo-motherland is involved in this industry of exported goods. Stitching and unstitching, somehow I want to leave that hole in the fabric, that hole which has punctured my heart as I hold these textures and folds which have been worn on my husband's body. As I turn to open the kitchen door and search for the thread in some drawer, all the ambivalences of time, capital, labour and love are undone and interlaced with guilt.

Yellow chalk on our wooden table outside. The words: *show love to others and be kind.* The world they will inherit is not fixed.

Another walk and I spy a *Vanessa atalanta.* Lurking behind the nets of an abandoned house are several butterfly squatters. Not caught by nets this time, just living within them. They inhabit the space between the net curtains and the panes of glass. I count four or five. Domesticated Red Admirals, which tells us it is spring. A few days later, the Indian actor Irrfan Khan dies and it is a shock because he is only in his early 50s. I remembered his performance in *The Lunchbox,* a film about a middle-aged man whose life is shaken by the arrival of a beautifully scented lunchbox and the woman who made its contents. Subtle, world-weary, knowing glances and quiet joy. I think of my mother cooking for my father and this invisible connection to home.

Now I cook for my mother, or order frozen meals to be delivered to her home. The children aren't allowed to embrace my mother anymore, not at first. When we moved, I moved her again, too, from her flat in Guildford to another in the centre of Exeter, but we were not expecting this moment. We wave to her from her window. In the summer, we take her out for tea. It will go on like this for a long time, but I still have to read her electricity meter, hoover the carpet, cut her hair. Her white hairs fall in strands on to the beige carpet in the flat. She fusses and tells me not to get it on her clothes. Eventually, we form a 'bubble', a unit, and are able to care for her more regularly. She even visits us, but now she cannot easily climb the stairs to the spare bedroom. She is 80.

Hallowe'en and a child stands in a pumpkin field. There are queues and cars parked up everywhere, all waiting to go and roll their wheelbarrows through the mud. Odd, bulbous shapes, circular and oval, mottled and torn, pulled from the soil. It is a fever dream in winter. Where is Sycorax? She is under the earth and in the trees, she is whispering behind your shoulder; her tears have filled these pumpkins and the water will never run dry. Yes, these pumpkins produce so much joy; the act of picking one is where the joy is born, yet this year, especially, it is so bittersweet. We are all living in an unclaimed harvest of life: so much on hold and postponed, an inertia which we push against, but cannot endure for much longer.

Damson

I want to be with those who know secret things
or else alone.

RAINER MARIA RILKE

She is winter's hollow, charcoal sketch or scrawl. On the
bitter grass, a ragged knot of rugged lashes. A deep-furrowed
brow, She sleeps.

Her back is a bridge, a ridge of mottled skin and ringed
flint. Broken, where once was summer's evergreen and now
stills the heartwood, the honeyed sap.

Hands upon hands, fingers loosen the loam. Spring-
bound. Levitating. We climb the tree.

Lightning struck this damson tree and now here we are,
a different volatility, feet and arms outstretched at its higher
and lighter ends. We plunder its shadow and tap the lichen
until it loosens. Light over the cottages. Fast through a thicket,
we fall. A set of rubber boots on the grass. A child's face and
the back of their head as they turn into the branches. Higher
and higher. The living things shift within its darkness and
entangle with the dead. *My father's ghost in the meadow.* The
branches make a gauze, a mesh through which to view the
world, a screen speckled with golden yellow moss; atomised
frames through which we peer, from high up, low down,
playing within their netted light.

To climb a tree, one must have faith in the weight of
things. A small branch might defeat you, and you shall fall.
Put your feet down, but remember you are not rooted here,
you are still moving. So, keep moving. Lightly, walk across
with the tips of your boots. Look for the places to hold. Look
for the places to fall. As you do this, your whole body will
move with the fibres of the tree; you are a wavelength and the

tree is the sound. Then, you have climbed a tree.

We inspect small green and pewter growths on the tree trunk, shredded and pierced through, perfect bullet holes. A wood beetle here, across my fingernail, and a thin worm on my boot. The smaller child squirms and jumps, giddy from the waves of movement. The older child is a blur of jacket and scarf between the zig-zag slivers, the outstretched branches bending at his will. Sharp and ridged, rough under their fingers, the bark crumbles and peels. My arms are balancing them as they drop down, one, two. *I'll catch you.*

They run across the meadow and tell me the grass is like the head of a kitchen mop or a medusa, like the jellyfish we saw at Exmouth beach. Childhood is a reservoir of happy memories which we carry into our future, into adulthood, as Helen Macdonald writes so movingly in her book *Vesper Flights.* The meadow of childhood's ever-glowing night turns inwards and folds itself into the future. A palimpsest, the mango orchard my father stole from in Rangoon is a thin outline whose flickering shape is projected beneath our meadow in Devon. My father's school days were his 'meadow', his reservoir of protected, restorative time and space; mine was in the shape of our garden where I made mud pies and watched the birds released from their aviary one summer's day.

With the valley in the distance and the little red-bricked cottages a stone's throw away, we enter this living and breathing playground and say hello to the chickens in their coop, the white and ginger cat (Willow) which often greets us and the damson tree which shelters all sorts of life forms.

I had been searching for this meadow. After nearly two years of life here in this hamlet, I had walked the lanes and the hedgerows and longed for open space which was not a field, not a yard. Then, I started to visit this small patch of land not far from our home and in the summer I saw that a neighbour had pitched a tent in its warm, long grass. Of course, it was here all along. We entered it and imagined we were camping. I walked out into the meadow and saw its microtopography, its tiny stories and visible life amongst the bark of the dead tree and the perfectly curving black branches of a willow tree. It was better than any lithographic print: a natural order and symmetry which is, of course, the way of all things living.

The other thing is the wind: the zephyr flight of leaves and dandelions, green beetles and catkins twirling. These currents of air fold outwards and whistle through my hair, which irritates my face and catches inside the collar of my jacket. The children chatter and howl in the wind. They are spellbound. Put your hand against a bracken, the winding lengths of a briar rose, or the wall of the barns, and you can feel the swelling, lashing of the wind and its gushing through your fingers. Watch the shuttling crescents of wind across the young barley. Sheep are statues weathering the storm. If you climb a tree, the wind will either steady your gait, spreading the force of gravity, or tempt you to bend to its will, curving, hunching your body when you should be still.

My father once climbed a mango tree. I climbed an apple tree in our garden in Hayes and fell, abruptly, winded. *How many years since I had climbed a tree?* I visit the meadow with the children and we try to name the things we see. I don't know the names of everything. We make new words for these arboreal beginnings, each sound growing out of the syllables of home and our living consciousness.

Yet, before there are new words, there are old ones to hold in our hearts. In my father's briefcase, I saw the word 'Shalimar' typed out on many of his documents: Shalimar, Howrah, the location of my aunt's first home in India and the home address on my father's boarding-school diary. I think of my aunt's voice saying this word with tenderness and my father's pronunciation, slightly different, with an emphasis on the fast sound of the 'sh' and a slower middle, his chin dropping to make the first 'a' sound a bit longer. The 'r' at the end is almost completely silent: 'Shaaalima-'. Shalimar was their home, but now its meaning floats free from its geographic location and becomes their legacy to me. Shalimar is the bridge between my father's world and my perception of it, not a real place but one of our own making, filled with his things, his stories, but also mine and my stories which are free for me to pass on as I go on without him. These stories will always migrate towards the place where we are now, *Shalimar*.

References

BOOKS

Ali, Salim and Ripley, S. D. (1996) *The Oxford Handbook of the Birds of India and Pakistan,* Oxford University Press

Aung San Suu Kyi (1995) *Freedom From Fear,* Penguin

Aung San Suu Kyi (1997) *Letters From Burma,* Penguin

Ballard, J. G. (1984) *Empire of the Sun,* Gollancz

Blythe, Ronald (1969) *Akenfield,* Penguin

Burnett, Elisabeth-Jane (2019) *The Grassling,* Penguin

Carroll, Lewis (1865) *Alice in Wonderland,* Macmillan

Chang, Jung (1991) *Wild Swans,* Harper Collins

Christie, Agatha (1937) *Death on the Nile,* Collins Crime Club

Clarke, Susanna (2004) *Jonathan Strange & Mr Norrell,* Bloomsbury

Darwin, Charles (1859) *On the Origin of Species,* John Murray

Dickens, Charles (1843) *A Christmas Carol,* Chapman and Hall

Gaita, Raimond (2003) *The Philosopher's Dog,* Routledge

Gaita, Raimond (1998) *Romulus, My Father,* Text Publishing Co

Hartley, L. P. (1953) *The Go-Between,* Hamish Hamilton

Hayes, Nick (2020) *The Book of Trespass,* Bloomsbury

Hodgson Burnett, Frances (1905) *A Little Princess,* Charles Scribner's Sons

Hodgson Burnett, Frances (1911) *The Secret Garden,* William Heinemann

Irigaray, Luce (1999) *The Forgetting of Air in Martin Heidegger,* University of Texas Press

Kerr, Judith (1968) *The Tiger Who Came to Tea,* Harper Collins

Khan-Din, Ayub (1999) *East is East,* Nick Hern Books

Kureishi, Hanif (1990) *The Buddha of Suburbia*, Faber and Faber

Kureishi, Hanif (1985) *My Beautiful Launderette*, Faber and Faber

Lee, Jessica J (2019) 'Pond: A Dendrochronology' in *At the Pond: Swimming at the Hampstead Ladies' Pond*, Daunt Books

Macdonald, Helen (2020) *Vesper Flights*, Jonathan Cape

Mayer, So, 'Introduction' in Rebecca Tamás and Sarah Shin (2019) *Spells: 21st Century Occult Poetry*, Ignota Press

Minghella, Anthony (1997) *The English Patient: A Screenplay*, Methuen Film

Oates, Eugene William (1889–1890) *The Fauna of British India, including Ceylon and Burma*, Taylor and Francis

Ondaatje, Michael (1997) *The English Patient*, McClelland & Stewart

Orwell, George (2001 edition) *Burmese Days*, Penguin

Overton, Jenny (1998) *A Suffragette Nest: Peaslake 1910 and After*, Hazeltree Publishing

Rilke, Rainer Maria (1905) *The Book of Hours*, Insel-Verlag

Roy, Arundhati (1997) *The God of Small Things*, Harper Collins

Shakespeare, William (*c.* 1611) *The Tempest*, Oxford University Press

Thomas, Dylan (1954) *Under Milk Wood*, New Directions

Waugh, Evelyn (1945) *Brideshead Revisited*, Penguin

Woolf, Virginia (1926) *On Being Ill*, Hogarth Press

MUSIC, FILM AND ARTWORKS

The Blue Boy (1770) Thomas Gainsborough

Career Girls (1997) Mike Leigh

Dance at Bougival (1883) Pierre-Auguste Renoir

Empire of the Sun (1987) Steven Spielberg

The Haywain (1821) John Constable

Indiana Jones and the Raiders of the Lost Ark (1981) Steven Spielberg

Infant (1929) Barbara Hepworth

The Lark Ascending (1914) Ralph Vaughan Williams

The Lunchbox (2013) Ritesh Batra

The Madness of King George (1994) Nicholas Hytner

Molly Drake Songs (2014) Tracey Thorn
Mothlight (1963) Stan Brakhage
Muriel's Wedding (1994) P. J. Hogan
My Fair Lady (1964) George Cukor
My Life Without Me (2003) Isabel Coixet
My Beautiful Launderette (1985) Stephen Frears
The Parting Cheer (1862) Henry Nelson O'Neil
Romulus, My Father (2007) Richard Roxburgh
Semele (1744) George Frideric Handel
Tiger in a Tropical Storm (Surprised!) (1891) Henri Rousseau

Acknowledgements

I wish to thank Lucy Bolton, Selwyn Boston, Elisabeth-Jane Burnett, Anna Cady, Sarah Cooper, Jemma Desai, Raimond Gaita, Michelle Williams Gamaker, Tony Grisoni, Fiona Handyside, Louise Hedges, Hoshi and Odette in Shere, Angela Huntingdon-Chown, Sonia Khan, Jackie and Mike Lack in Peaslake, Jessica J. Lee, So Mayer, Victoria Millar, James Miller, Holly Ovenden, Angela Piccini, Anna Backman Rogers, Mohsen Shah and Emma Wilson. I am grateful to Michael Ondaatje for allowing me to quote their work, and to *Litro* for their enthusiasm for the first piece I ever wrote, which evolved into the first section of this book. Without the guidance and wisdom of Adrian, Gracie, Jon and Graham at Little Toller, this book might never have existed; my agent Philippa Sitters, at David Godwin, has also offered up solid support and advice (plus most ebullient Instagrams in lockdown). Thanks also to Jessica Woollard and Susannah Godman.

I have written this book for Lambert Quinlivan, my mother, Patricia, my uncle David Duncan, Richard Martino, Adelaide Martino, Inigo, Orlando, Dylan and Loretta.

D. Q.
DEVON, 2022